Metta Victoria Fuller Victor

Lives of Female Mormons

A narrative of facts stranger than fiction

Metta Victoria Fuller Victor

Lives of Female Mormons
A narrative of facts stranger than fiction

ISBN/EAN: 9783337295165

Printed in Europe, USA, Canada, Australia, Japan

Cover: Foto ©ninafisch / pixelio.de

More available books at **www.hansebooks.com**

LIVES OF FEMALE MORMONS;

A NARRATIVE OF

FACTS STRANGER THAN FICTION.

BY

METTA VICTORIA FULLER.

"Here is light on the sea and land,
And the dream deceives nevermore."

PHILADELPHIA:

PUBLISHED BY G. G. EVANS,

NO. 439 CHESTNUT STREET.

1860.

INTRODUCTION

THE following narrative tells its own sad tale; but will its moral sink deeply in the hearts of the people of this Union who are now called upon to admit Deseret into this brotherhood of States? The people of Utah, strengthened by numbers until the population now reaches upward of 77,000 inhabitants, have prepared their Constitution, and will, ere this work reaches the hands of the reader, have presented it to Congress, asking for admission as a State. Ere that admission is granted we conjure every man who has respect for humanity and for progress, to pause over this little record of *one* history, and then, multiplying it by tens of thousands, say if he can find it in his heart to fellowship with such a moral monster as Deseret now is, and will continue to be under the laws and Constitution which she has prescribed for herself.

A crisis has come in our affairs which it is as painful to contemplate as the slow march of a disease which threatens to desolate all households. Men are armed against men—State legislates against State—violence obtrudes into our legislative halls, *once* sacred to the people's representatives—men are pronounced "incendiaries," "enemies of their kind," "traitors," and the physical force of the bayonet and cannon-ball has come to quell the first outbreak of passion. Like the baffled sea, the waves for a moment recede, only to come leaping with a more terrible force to the shore, then moan, and beat, and rage, until that barrier gives way, and the fair land is given up to the frightful deluge. It becomes citizens of America to pause before that rising storm, and to see if there be not oil for the troubled waters.

Under the principles of sovereignty embodied in the Kansas-Nebraska Act, any Territory with a republican Constitution and a sufficient number of inhabitants, can come into this Union of States. The social and internal regulations of such State are to be ordered as the people, by popular vote, shall decree. Upon its face this seems a just enactment; but, looking beneath, to its eventual operation, we see that the principle is one dangerous to the stability and progress of the country, detrimental to the individual State and to the individuals of such State. For, under its operation, Utah is entitled to enjoy unmolested her polygamy and slavery; and thus the Constitution of the United States, which regards all men free and equal, fosters two as great wrongs as now disgrace the civilized world. We ask, as Americans, are we willing that *such* a construction should be placed upon that Constitution ?

The institution of slavery in a free government is a paradox, and gives the lie to the professions the authors of this republic made, else have we shamefully perverted their gifts—which, it is not hard to say. Territory which *they* pledged to be FREE has been overshadowed by the darkness of African servitude— the political influence of such an institution has grown apace with each additional State adopting negro "property" as a basis of representation in Congress—and thus has the free government of our fathers become but free in form, to protect a tyranny such as no civilized-nation on the face of this earth would tolerate. The responsibility of such a perversion rests with the degenerate sons of noble sires, and the future will not fail to fasten the record where it belongs.

This we say in no spirit of enmity to the South, nor of undue reproach to the North: it is from the love we bear to that blessed Constitution, earned by the blood of our fathers, and ..the tears and sufferings of our mothers; and we appeal to their children to stay their tongues long enough for thought and prayer; to stay the passion which governs them, to see if they are not in the wrong, in the advocacy, directly, or indirectly through the "squatter sovereignty" principle, of what their better sense knows to be wrong, degrading, dangerous to happiness, fatal to all true progress and true liberty.

Repulsive as slavery appears to us, we can but deem polygamy a thing more loathsome and poisonous to social and political purity. Half-civilized States have ceased its practice as dangerous to happiness, and as outraging every instinct of the better nature within every breast; and as ages rolled away they left the institution behind as one of the relics of barbarism which marked the half-developed state of man as a social being. Its last remaining shadow now rests upon the Turk, and he, profiting by the example of his sultan, is gradually casting it aside, and soon will stand forth as a monogamist. And thus it bade fair to die out, and woman and society bade fair to come forth clad in a nobility of moral purity, which should, indeed, seem like the livery of heaven. Who could have prophesied that in republican America the lie should be given to that promise, and that the atrocity, protected by the strong arm of government, should become once more a power for evil?

The American people, absorbed in their grand schemes of physical development, are apt to shut their eyes to the moral aspects of their society. This moral apathy it is which has allowed the system of slavery to grow and expand until it is now fast becoming the controling element in the government; and this apathy it is which would allow the introduction of polygamy into American institutions to become one of the elements of our society. Who shall be to blame if that instrument of barbarism becomes linked to our country, protected by its army and navy, by its Constitution, by its moral force and sympathy? Let us not be deceived longer, but open our eyes to the serpent now asking to be warmed into life by our national hearth-stone; let us arise and say, "Away leper! cleanse thyself! and then come, and we will gladly receive thee into our household—will then gladly give thee equal share in our councils—then will protect thee as our fathers protected Bunker's Hill? Away with thee, and cleanse thyself!"

Reject Deseret, and we accomplish the first step in a reform which shall restore our country to its once proud purity, and give to it a new character for moral and intellectual grandeur. Under its laws we ought to be the best, the purest, the wisest, the bravest people on earth; and this we shall be are we but true to the first principles laid down by our Revolutionary fathers—the nobility of man. Whatever degrades him—whatever corrupts and injures his moral, intellectual, and physical well-being is inimical to the well-being of society, to the State, to the whole country; consequently, to the spirit and intent of that Constitution which is to perpetuate the republic, and render it, in truth, the refuge for the oppressed, the *home* of liberty. And, as citizens of this country, we owe it as a duty, not only to the Constitution, but to humanity, that we sternly oppose slavery in all its forms—intemperance and its hideous deformities, and polygamy with its train of evils which no man can truly conceive, but which surely will end in animalizing man, in corrupting the very founts of virtue and purity, and, finally, in barbarism. Reject Deseret, we say, as the first step in this great reform—refuse to her the sympathy and equality of the old and long-tried commonwealths—compel her to cast away her overshadowing sin, and then shall we have assurance that our hearts are still right, and hopes that our country will come out of the present threatening crisis purified, strengthened, full of life, and well-fitted to accomplish our mission of initiating the true republic.

———

We may be permitted to quote from the Philadelphia "North American and United States Gazette" the following, not only as "food for thought," but as embodying suggestions which will serve as a basis for action in the present contingency:

"Among a party of nine hundr\.d Mormons, who recently left comfortable homes in England, to surrender themselves to the sway of Brigham Young and his hopeful associates, came two girls, whose transfer to the Utah land of abominations has very much the character of kidnapping. The story of their flight, as related in the English papers, is as follows: Their father was a man in middle life, well to do and industrious. His labors had placed his family, consisting of a wife and several children, in a state of decent competence and happiness. Satan came among them in the guise of a Mormon emissary, and beguiled the eldest son, who made a pilgrimage to the land of rogues. True to their instincts, the crafty elders of Salt Lake made Mormonism so delightful to the neophyte, and advanced him so rapidly in their fraternity, that he returned to England as a preacher of the delusion. The father, whose employment took him away from his family for periods of a week at a time, returned to the house one Saturday from a business excursion, to find it deserted. His whole family had disappeared, with whatever portables they could lay hands upon; and his wife had stolen his money to no inconsiderable amount—all that she could collect or pilfer. He traced the fugitives to Liverpool, and reached that place to discover that they had embarked, under the persuasions of his Mormon son, in

an emigrant ship, the *Enoch Train*. The distracted
father chartered a steam-tug, and taking with him a
police officer, overtook the vessel. After an infinite
deal of persuasion, aided by the master of the ship,
and opposed by the Mormon leaders, he succeeded in
inducing his wife to go back with him. He also, as
a matter of great favor, obtained the surrender of
his .infant children. But his two eldest daughters
refused to return with their parents, and the heart-
broken father went without them. Their fate, going
thus unprotected to Utah, may well cause a shudder.

" A community thus replenished is maturing meas-
ures to apply for admission as one of the States of
this confederacy. We were never among those who
'calculated the value of the Union,' or who dreamed
that the possibility of its being sundered was among
contingencies to be considered in any case. But the
possibility that our fathers may have fought to es-
tablish a shield for a community of adulterers and
bigamists, and their progeny, makes us pause. That
all which we hold sacred in religion, or virtuous in
social and family relations, may be trampled under-
foot by a State represented on equal terms with those
founded by Penn and the Pilgrims, by Oglethorpe and
the Cavaliers; that the Old Dominion and the land of
the Puritans may be allied with a fraternity of licen-
tious and debauched rogues—these possibilities, should

they become facts, will leave no value to the Union
for any body to 'calculate.' Nothing has cast so
great a doubt over the future of this country as the
Mormon plague spot. And if the State of Utah is to
be admitted into our constellation, the sign will lose
its present proud significance, and stand—as stars
sometimes do, in an equivoque—the representatives of
something too foul to be spoken or written.

"And all this evil, if it be consummated, will
be fairly chargeable upon the absurdity of squatter
sovereignty—a demagogue's figment to serve a party
purpose, carried to its legitimate deductions by knaves,
operating through the instrumentality of zealots, fan-
atics, fools, and lechers. We have no patience with
the Mormons, and as little with temporisers who leave
the evil to increase, until at last literal and bloody war
may be forced upon us to crush what common sense
and a just idea of the powers of the general government might have averted. The contact with the
Mormons of such settlers of the West as have just
ideas of purity and decency, will be terrible whenever
the tide of emigration reaches them. And if the
descendants of the wretches now wallowing in Mormonism—modern vermin perpetuating their kind in
the disgusting ratio of other loathsome creatures—if,
we say, these children of such paternity do not form a
Pariah race in our country, it will be because this bad

leaven taints the whole moral mass. Extremes meet. We have enjoyed a high order of social virtue in this republican country, because no corrupt royalty and nobility have made illegitimacy tolerable, and recommended the bend sinister as a badge of honor, provided that the blood, no matter by what questionable vein it descends, be ' honorable.'   But if squatter sovereignty, and liberty deteriorating into licentiousness, produce the same results, we have only substituted Fitz-Youngs and Fitz-Mormons for Fitz-Jameses and Fitz-Clarences; and certainly have not gained much by the exchange."

MORMON WIVES.

CHAPTER I.

"Bring flowers, fresh flowers, for the bride to wear!
They were born to blush in her shining hair.
She is leaving the home of her childhood's mirth!
She hath bid farewell to her father's hearth;
Her place is now by another's side—
Bring flowers for the locks of the fair young bride."

Mrs. Hemans.

It was the first day of June, and Margaret Fletcher's wedding-day. She was to be married in the evening, and all the afternoon she sat alone in her chamber. It was a small, low room in the upper half-story of the old farm house; but it was pleasant despite of its smallness. Its window looked over the rose-bushes and pinks in the front yard, across the road, to the meadow and woodland beyond, and to the blue line of the sea lying in the distance. Within, all wore that look of order and neatness which spoke the purity of the maiden's tastes. The curtains of dimity at the window and

around the toilet-table were newly hung and deco-
rated with sprays of myrtle and rose-buds. The
fine linen pillow-casings and handsome counter-
panes were exquisitely white; a dress of snowy
Indian lawn, a pair of satin slippers, and two or
three simple adornments for the robe lay upon
the bed. Guiltless of a knowledge of French per-
fumery, Margaret had strewn rose-leaves over the
bridal attire and throughout the room.

She sat at the casement, her head leaned into her
hand, looking off in the direction of the ocean, but
seeing only the dream-land of the future in which
her thoughts were wandering.

Clouds drifted up over the declining sun, throwing a shadow upon the landscape which startled
Margaret. She thought it later than it was, and
arose to dress for the ceremony. She had no
sisters to aid her at this pleasant task, and she had
not asked any of her companions in the neighbor-
hood to be her bridemaids. Slowly and still, as
if half-lost in reverie, she arranged her dark brown
hair. Three or four long, shining curls dropped
down beside either cheek and lay against her beautiful neck; the rest were gathered into a simple knot

behind. Her fingers rested idly when this was
done, and she stood looking into the reflection of
her own earnest eyes until the voices of two or
three relatives, coming through the yard, again reminded her that she must hasten.

The clouds were sweeping more darkly now over
the sky, and it was twilight, although the sun had
not set. In a few moments the slender foot was in
its satin slipper, and the soft folds of the snowy
lawn waved airily about the youthful form. Margaret was one of the most beautiful of those fair
New England maidens, who grow up amid the hills
and chilly breezes as sweetly and delicately as
Alpine roses. She had been reared in seclusion
upon the farm, and on the homestead where she
was born; but no lady of the fashionable world
had a more dainty repose of manner, a more stately
carriage, or a gentler beauty. Suddenly the sun,
the moment before his setting, shone through a rift
in the thick clouds, deluging the little chamber
with floods of crimson light. But it was not the
red of the sunset tinging Margaret's cheek. The .
step, the voice of the bridegroom she heard from
the door below, and her whole being became ra-

diant in the glowing light. A warm color rushed
into her face, her eyes drooped, and the fingers,
which were fastening a white rose in the bosom of
her dress, refused to accomplish their task. It
seemed as if the rosy hue which tinged her bridal
dress was caught from her face and bosom instead
of from the lustrous sky.

Some one tapped at her chamber-door. She
thought it was her mother, and tried to overcome
the rapid beating of her heart, as she said, "Come in!"

"Sarah Irving! how come *you* here?" she exclaimed in surprise, as a girl of about her own age
entered the room and stood, half embarrassed, half
defiant, before her.

"As you did not invite me, I thought I would
ask myself to the wedding," replied her visitor,
forcing a smile into the brilliant dark eyes, which
looked as if their owner had ways of her own for
accomplishing her will, even when it did clash with
conventionalities.

"It was your own fault that you were not in-
vited, Sarah ; but I am very glad to see you, if you
have come in good faith."

"I know that it was my own fault—all my own

fault, dear Margaret; and it is just like you to forgive me, even before I have made apologies. It
was a childish mood of coldness I took toward you.
I ought to be treated like a child—scolded, and par-
doned. It is all past now, and I have to try to be
worthy of your former friendship. See I have
brought you a wedding-present."

She took from her own dress an old-fashioned
brooch, set with costly pearls, and fastened with
it the rose upon Margaret's breast.

"Why, Sarah, I must not accept that! I know
how highly you prize it as a family treasure; it is
too rich a gift. Keep it for your own wedding, my
dear friend."

Sarah laughed a quick, bitter laugh.

"I shall never be married; so keep my offering,
or I shall be offended."

It was a strange assertion for one so young and
beautiful to make with such sharp earnestness. So
Margaret thought, as she looked affectionately into
her perturbed face.

"Never be married!" she said, with a smile. "I
hope you will not, until, like me, you have met
the man whom you can not help obeying when he

commands you to unsay that. As for your being
offended at me—it will not be the first time; however, I wish to run no risks; so I accept your
beautiful gift, and with double delight because it
comes from you."

"They are waiting for you down stairs; the
minister has arrived," said Sarah, hurriedly putting
by Margaret's kiss of thanks ; "let me see, I do not
believe I have brushed my hair to-day."

She gave a passing glance into the mirror. Her
hair was indeed rather carelessly arranged, but it
was beautiful however it might chance to fall.
She almost started back from the intense brilliancy
of her own eyes.

"It will have to do," she said, taking her companion's arm; "dear! how red my cheeks are—red
as poppies!"

The two girls passed down the staircase together.
They had been friends from infancy; at school
they had chosen each other as confidantes; they
were neighbors; and they had grown up without
any serious misunderstandings, although Sarah,
with her passionate temperament, sometimes took
freaks of anger or jealousy.

Margaret was the most patient, loving, and forgiving of the two. Sarah could rely upon her generous, placid goodness, even when her own whims deserved resentment. She often wounded her needlessly, but her own remorse would be so keen—she would cast herself back upon her friend's love with a humility so touching in one so proud, that it was far from Margaret's deeply tender heart not to forgive her.

This last coldness of hers had been of a more serious nature. About three months gone she had adopted a reserved, even repulsive manner; so that Margaret, after some attempts at an explanation, and some secret tears, gave over all effort to reconcile a difficulty when she was ignorant of any cause of offense. She grieved over this separation less than she might otherwise have done, as, about that time, she became engaged to Richard Wilde, and all other feelings were absorbed in the love she felt for him. Often, when she sat in her chamber preparing her wedding-garments, or thought in solitude over her strange happiness, she wished for Sarah to share in this new and wonderful joy; but again her feelings would seem to

her so sacred and beyond expression, that not even
her friend's old sympathy could be trusted with
them. And when she was in Richard's presence,
then she forgot a wish for any one else in the
world. The music of his rich voice, the spell in
the light of his deep gray eye, fascinated her
every thought and sense.

It was one of the wonders of the earth to her that
any one could say a word against Richard. She
thought all must yield to the sweet influence of his
smile, and the magic which lurked in his subtle and
flashing glance, as readily as she. He *was* a winning man to the most of people; though he excited
that doubt and remark, and sometimes that dislike
which people who can not be entirely comprehended
are apt to provoke. His mind was of cultivation
and capacity beyond that of any other in the quiet
village where he resided. His studies as a lawyer
in the office of his father, old Squire Wilde, the
resources of the family library, and his own inquir-
ing, restless disposition, forever prying into the
meaning of things, had made him not only intelligent but ambitious. Twice he had left home and
wandered abroad for a year or two, partly seeking

for a situation where the powers he felt within him might be developed, and partly satisfying his craving to know all about the world of men and objects. Both times he had returned without any particular result in the eyes of his neighbors, except an increased faculty for making himself entertaining by the variety of knowledge he contrived to communicate in his conversation. And another charge was whispered with awe and incredulity by the pious and faithful inhabitants of that Puritan village. From his neglecting almost entirely to attend worship, and from some sneering remarks which he had made about their forms and ceremonies, it had come to be rumored that he was "an unbeliever." This was the only shadow upon Margaret's happiness.

She did not believe, as many of her neighbors did, that he was an atheist or an infidel. She had questioned him closely; and he had avowed his faith that there was a God of goodness and love who controlled the universe, and that men should be governed by the precepts of Christ

"But he could not give his heart," he said, "to the hollow forms of their chilling doctrines; he,

3

despised the self-righteous sanctimoniousness of many of their deacons and ministers; he believed that the Church stood in the way of progress; he believed that he could accomplish more good not to be fettered by her chains."

Margaret could not but grieve and shed tears at this; for to her, reared in all the rigidness of the old Puritan school, such avowals seemed not only wrong and dangerous, but positively wicked. Yet Richard was not wicked! His doctrines might be, but he was not. He was charitable, he bore no malice, he was kind to the poor, he praised God, with a full heart at times, when he was lost in admiration of His works. Oh, no! when she compared him with some of the envious, avaricious, cold-hearted men who held high places in the Church of which she was a member, she excused his words, his mistaken doubts, upon the plea that his heart was all right.

It was more difficult to convince her parents of this. In a worldly view, Richard Wilde was an excellent match for their daughter; but they had her real interests too deeply at heart to be willing to give her up to "an unbeliever." He reasoned with them more earnestly than he had done with Margaret; and, too, he made concessions, more than he could have done with perfect candor. But he loved their child, and he could not lose her upon a misunderstanding or a difference in religious matters. Upon his promising to attend church for six months regularly, and to *try* and open his soul to conviction, they gave their otherwise pleased consent to the union.

Richard Wilde smiled—he could not help it—as he walked home after that interview, at the idea of *his* sitting for six months under the preaching of an ignorant and dogmatic minister, whose whole logic and argument he had long ago at his fingers' ends.

"It is but a concession to the feelings of those who love me," he said to himself, in extenuation of his want of perfect truth. "I need not refuse what will, after all, be but a trifling sacrifice of my comfort, since I am to sit by the side of my beautiful Margaret. He may drag his sermons out an hour and a half every Sabbath if I am to have Margaret nestled in the same pew—my wife."

The last charmed word plunged him into a sea

of dreams, where his fancy floated upon blissful wings.

"God bless you, Margaret, my child, and make you as happy in the new relation as your mother has been. Twenty-five years your father and I have dwelt together, and we are dearer to each other this moment than when we were first pronounced man and wife. A mother's blessing I give you, my daughter," said Mrs. Fletcher, coming out to meet the girls as they descended the stairs, and taking Margaret in her trembling arms.

A few tears dropped from the young girl's eyes as she kissed her mother's cheeks. But Richard had come out, too, and was gazing upon her with eyes of passionate admiration. She saw all the love, the exultation of his air, although she gave him but a half glance; then, her cheeks suffused with blushes, and her eyes yet bright with tears, she gave him her hand, and he led into the large, old-fashioned parlor, where a few relatives only were assembled.

Lamps had been lighted, displaying bouquets in the china vases upon the mantel, and wreaths over the windows and mirror.   The guests were too intent upon the entrance of the bride and bridegroom, to notice how sultry the air had grown, or how suddenly a hot wind came up, blowing a cloud of fragrant rose-leaves in at the casement, and making a hoarse murmur amid the trees upon the lawn.

The blushes died from Margaret's cheeks when the ceremony began: she stood, pale and earnest, making, in a low voice, the customary replies.   The minister had not finished his blessing, when a crash of thunder, so terribly near and unsuspected that all were startled, interrupted him.   The bride trembled and clung to her husband, but soon recovered from the brief terror, and turning her glance upon her friend Sarah, was surprised to see her deathly white, and her eyes fixed upon vacancy.

"Speak to her, mother," she entreated Mrs. Fletcher, who came up to give her the first greeting.

"Why, Sarah, are you ill? are you frightened?" exclaimed the mother, laying her hand upon her shoulder to arouse her.

"I am neither—neither; I believe I was a little shocked," was the gay reply; and the young girl sprang to her feet with a mocking laugh.   "The thunder has seen fit to salute you; let me do you like honor," and she shook hands with the newly-married pair.

They felt that her hands were icy cold, and that there was something remarkable in her manner; but she was a creature of impulse and wild behavior, and they thought no more of it.

One of those sudden storms common at that season of the year, had broken upon the night, and was spending its fury as it passed over. Peal after peal of sharp thunder rattled around; but none was so startling as the first. The company soon regained composure—going out gayly to the supper-room to partake of the dainties which had been spread for them.

"I wonder what has become of Sarah Irving? she ought to have a chance toward obtaining the ring," exclaimed one of Margaret's young brothers, as the bride-cake went the rounds.

One or two of the youths went to the parlor in search of her, but she was not to be found. She had fled away into the night and tempest. Unable any longer to brook the happiness of the marriage-feast, she had dashed out into the wind and rain, braving the elements, in her thin dress, careless of or defying danger. By the glare of the lightning she found her way home; drenched and miserable she crept to her room, sitting by the window until the storm without doors and the storm in her own heart were somewhat wearied out.

CHAPTER II.

"Unwise and most unfortunate
My way was; let the sign—
The proof of it—be simply this,
Thou art not, wert not mine!"

PINCKNEY.

WITHIN a week or two after their marriage,
Margaret went to housekeeping in the village of
S——, which was only about two miles from the
old homestead. Richard's father gave him a handsome house standing in the midst of a couple of
acres of cultivated garden and lawn. Four or
five stately elms kept guard before the grass-plot,
honeysuckles and roses clambered over the por-
ticoes: it was as sweet a place as "young love"
need desire for his first beginning in domestic
life. Margaret's parents had given her *carte blanche*
to furnish the mansion as her taste dictated; and
simply and cheerfully, not with garish display,
was it fitted up. A beautiful piano was the
richest article the parlor could boast—a new piano,

for the mother would not let the old one be taken away : she wanted Margaret to play for them when she came home, which must be very often. The profuse supply of household linen which had long been hoarded up for her, and which the bride received as a part of her portion, might have awak-ened the envy of less comfortably supplied begin-ners.

Like many of the unequalled New England girls, she could not only cull exquisite music from the piano, but she understood all the mysteries and du-ties of neat and economical housekeeping. She had a good servant in the kitchen ; and it was a pleasure for her to superintend all the arrangements, and even to execute the lightest daily tasks ; while she still had abundance of leisure to bestow upon the small society of the village, upon her music, and always, time to run and meet her husband, to smooth her curls, and put fresh roses in her hair and on her cheeks for his coming, to sing for him, to talk with him, to make him happy.

Richard had gone into the office with his father as partner in his law business. There seemed noth-ing in the way of this young couple's leading a life of peculiar prosperity, blessed as they were with a competency, health, beauty, intelligence and love.

True to his promise, Richard went every Sabbath to church, and sat by the side of his beautiful bride with a face of sufficient gravity to please the most sanctimonious. Not that he was hypocritical about that: he was a mocker of the Church but not of God; and when he heard His name, or went to the place dedicated, however farcical he might deem it, to His presence, he observed a propriety of demeanor. But he did not spare the minister and deacons. If Margaret asked him, after reaching home, how he liked the sermon, his reply was either a ludicrous and sarcastic criticism upon the good man's effort, or a—"Really, darling, I did not hear it, indeed I did not; I was lost in reverie; I was thinking of you, wife, a much more interesting occupation than listening; and the old man's eloquence fell upon my ear like the distant murmur of ocean waves upon a senseless shore."

Sometimes tears of reproach would bedew Margaret's eyes, and then he would soften what he had said with kisses, and love her more tenderly than ever; for the most reckless man likes to see a woman religious, even if her faith takes the shape of prejudice.

Among the most frequent of Margaret's visitors was her own brother Harry, a pleasant-appearing young man about two years older than herself, and her friend Sarah Irving. She loved to fancy that they came there to meet each other. She had but little doubt that Harry had yielded his heart into the keeping of her beautiful friend; she did not see how he could resist, pure-hearted and innocent of art as he was. The influence of Sarah's thousand charms and graces, all the more fascinating that they were touched with the fire of her peculiar nature, as a southern flower is warmed and tinged by a southern sun. She was the most accomplished and brilliant girl whom Harry had ever met, and knowing her from childhood, while her intimacy with his sister gave him every opportunity to see her and be near her, it might be expected that she had grown to be the ideal of all womanly loveliness to him.

Almost every evening during the summer of the wedding he was at Margaret's house, who could not fail to notice that if Sarah was absent,

not even her music which he professed to come
to hear, could win him from his abstracted mood.
If the young girl was there, and gave him one arch
smile or one playful glance of her bright eyes,
or one flashing ebullition of wit however much at
his expense, he seemed content. For was there
not always the long walk home with her, alone
beneath the evening sky? and the saying good-
night at the door—always simply "good-night;"
though each evening he would resolve that at the
next he would add some tell-tale word or beg a
precious boon beside. Yet something in her manner restrained him, sending him on the other mile
which he had to walk in solitude, not always de-
spondingly, but more often with that feeling of
love and awe which dwells in the heart of a pure-
minded man toward the woman whom he has not
yet won to confess a preference for him.

As the weeks glided by, Margaret grew to be
less contented with the state of affairs. There was
something about Sarah which she could not understand. Hitherto, although it was stirred by wild
and capricious winds of fancy and passion, whenever her spirit was at rest, Margaret could see to

the very bottom of its clear, bright waters, and love their fairness; but now, even when not tossed by unexpected moods into sparkle or gloom, it was ruled by a cold, impenetrable mist.

She began to mistrust that Sarah did not and never would return the passion of her brother, which was growing every day more away from his power to conceal it. She felt a small degree of sisterly indignation when she looked upon the earnest face of Harry, pale sometimes with repressed feeling, and noted how all his deep solicitude was met with the same gayety, untouched with the softness of emotion.

"If she should trifle with him," she thought to herself; "but no, Sarah will never be guilty of heartlessness. It is but the coquetry natural to a proud young girl. Her soul will be melted, as mine has been; she will find it sweeter to yield to a noble affection than to make sport of it."

Thus the weeks glided on, and in time Henry became restless and uneasy; the fever of an unavowed passion was consuming his soul; there grew a shadow, and beneath it a brightness in his

3

blue eyes; and the frank smile that dwelt upon his lip became fitful and rare. Yet still Sarah came day after day to the house of his sister, as if on purpose to meet him; still she laughed earnestly, played music that was "dancing mad," and her eyes shot glances of fire from beneath the covert of their long lashes. One hour she would bewilder them with her bright, invulnerable gayety; and the next sit silent and dark—beautiful as evening, and as sad. Then it would seem as if the tenderness yearning in the heart of the young man must burst forth; yet to him, even in her stillness, she was unapproachable as a star No one knew whether she was acting out merely her untamed girlish impulses, or whether some secret spring was moving her spirit—no one but Richard Wilde, and he only suspected that he had the key to her actions

"What do you think has come over Sarah?" his wife asked him one night, after the young couple were on their way home.

Sarah had been in one of her most wilful moods, and had grieved Margaret, astonished Richard, and wounded Harry; so that he had offered to escort her home with great coldness, and she had accepted his services as haughtily.

"She was always a will-o'-the-wisp, and I am afraid that she will never be any thing better."

"Oh, no! Richard, she is wayward, I know; but I do believe that there is depth and truth enough in her nature to make a noble woman of her yet; 'with all her faults I love her still.'"

"If there is any truth in her, I wish that she would not trifle with Harry any longer. It is no better than murder for a woman to do what she is doing; keeping a loving heart stretched on the rack of her coquetry," replied Richard, with unusual sternness.

"Yet how sweet she is, how affectionate, how gentle at times! She was so faithful to me when I was ill a year ago, Richard; she never left me; and she is just as kind at home to her family. They worship her; and indeed I love her all the more for her wildness, I think often."

"Well, let Harry win his mocking-bird if he can. I would rather have my nightingale that sings always the same sweet song;" and the young husband turned the face of his wife toward the light as he kissed her, for he loved to see the delicate color steal into her cheek, which still came at a word of praise from him.

"Sarah is very beautiful," he said the next moment.

"And it is a beauty all her own; I never saw any one like her," answered Margaret.

"She has fire and sweetness enough in her eyes to entrance a stone, when she is in her happiest moods," continued Richard. "I do not wonder that Harry is tangled in her spell. If I were him I would not wait a day—no, nor an hour, until I would have my fate decided for better or worse. She would not keep *me* dancing attendance upon her pleasure: I could not endure it, and I would not."

"I always thought Harry had pride enough," sighed his sister.

"But when men or women are in love, there is no telling in what strange directions their passion will develop itself. I presume I acted with all the customary foolishness, did n't I, Maggie, before you promised me?"

"*I* never saw any thing foolish about you," said

Margaret, with such a pretty earnestness that her husband laughed.

The next day, as Mr. and Mrs. Wilde were sitting upon the front portico, enjoying a cool breeze which had arisen, and the sunset clouds that were glowing in the west, Sarah came from the street up the garden-walk. Her bonnet was swinging on her arm, and the wind was blowing her curls about her face. She came along slowly, looking a little pale, and there was an unusual timidity in her aspect.

"I behaved so badly last night," she said, in a low voice, taking a seat upon the steps at their feet, "I wonder how any of my friends can love me; I can not love myself."

How much more beautiful she looked in that moment of humility than when in her dazzling moods. Margaret inly wished that Harry could see her as she sat there with her eyes cast down. He did see her. He had been with them to tea, and was standing in the shelter of the curtains at the window opening upon the portico, when she came up. He was gazing upon her almost with suspended breath; and the soft voice of her con-

4

fession fell upon his perturbed spirits like a sweet
calm. All day he had been distressed, not only
with doubts of whether she would listen to his
suit, but also with fears that if he should win her,
her variable disposition would render him unhappy.

The touching gentleness of her present appearance banished every such wise reflection; and he
longed to tell her that there was one at least whose
love could not be turned away, even by her mockery of it.

"You seem born to do what you please with
people," replied Margaret, affectionately. "You are
a queen in your own right; and I do not think you
mean to be a very cruel one, though occasionally
you exercise your power in a despotic manner."

"Who can not govern themselves should not
aspire to rule others," said the young girl; "but,
indeed, I am going to do better hereafter. I have
been afflicted with a strange malady for the past
few months; but the disease is conquered now, I
am sure, and I shall soon be convalescent. Then
you will have the Sarah that you used to have
again, only chastened by her experience in suffering."

She spoke in a grave voice; and her dark eyes looked away into the burning depths of the sunset with an unspeakable sadness and yearning. She looked like one who had achieved a victory, and was yet worn with the struggles—serene and yet melancholy.

Never before had the heart of Harry Fletcher gone out to her with such fullness of tenderness; and yet her words had given him a sharp pain. *What* worm had been silently preying upon the bloom of her heart? What was the nature of her past sorrow? Was it one to which he could not minister? which would widen the space between them—had she loved another, and in vain, and he never suspecting it? The fear was a new one; for she had treated all her admirers so much more coldly even than she had treated him, that he had felt there was not at least *that* bar to his success in winning her. He was both mystified and pained. One thing he resolved upon before he moved a fold of the curtain by which he was concealed: he would no longer endure this suspense— he would hear his fate from her lips that night; no caprice which she might put on should repel

him. And, oh! what a wild hope he had—the
deepest hope of a life-time—that he might break
down the barriers which divided their souls, and
drawing that face, so sweet, so pale in the solemn
sunset light, to his bosom, hear from those lips
that they would be kind to him, would repulse
him no more, would breathe their sweetness both
of grief and joy to him.

As he stood thus, with his soul illuminating his
fine features, he looked manly enough to be the
lover of a very high-hearted woman. He was but
a country youth. Two or three years spent stud-
iously in college had been his only experience
away from home. But he had the native grace
of a gentleman, and full enough personal beauty
to set off his more noble qualities. The natural
purity of his heart had not been polluted by fashionable dissipations; his keen sense of honor was
such as sometimes to reflect upon the less scrupu-
lous impulses of his brother-in-law. The girl beloved by him ought to have been happy in the
confidence that she was enriched by an affection
which would be life-long, and by the companionship of a generous and gentle spirit; but "the

wind bloweth where it listeth," and love obeys no known laws.

A few more remarks were exchanged by the friends upon the portico, which Harry did not hear—he was too deeply absorbed in the resolution he had made. He stepped out by her side, and gave the greetings of the evening to Sarah. The sad serenity of her eyes gave way to a troubled look after meeting his glance ; her feminine intuitions betrayed to her something of what was in his thought.

"I must go home," she said, presently, "before it grows dark."

"Why not stay ?" asked Margaret.

"I have a new piece of music, and I feel like playing it to-night. I did not intend to spend the evening. Good-night, all."

But Harry would not take her hint that she needed no company. "I must see you safely home, Miss Irving."

"Oh, no, I thank you. I can reach home before night; and I have gone later than this a thousand times."

"Our paths lie in the same direction, Sarah, and

so I shall walk beside you," he said, coming **down**
the steps and joining her.

They bade the others good-night, and passed
along, Harry inly wondering if their paths for life
were to lie in the same direction, and firmly resolved to ascertain, without any more of the dangers of delay. For several moments there was
silence between them, until they had passed the
village street, and were out on the country-road.
Then Sarah began talking vivaciously, as if to prevent her companion from broaching any more serious subject.

"If there's a music in the world which I love,"
said she, "it is this soft murmur of the wind in the
tree-tops. When that little bird, dropping to its
nest, broke in just now, with that clear, quick war-
ble, its effect upon me was as if a sunbeam had suddenly fallen upon a smoothly-gliding stream—the
flowing of the continuous undertone, and on its
bosom those glancing, sparkling notes. This av-
enue of elms is very beautiful, don't you think so?"

"Very beautiful, Sarah; but there is something
which I—"

"And that faint line of crimson in the western

sky : I would that it were a boat, and I sailing
about through that golden sea.   By the way, Harry,
did you know that Miss Green is to give a party
this week ?"

"I do not care any thing about Miss Green's
party," said the young man, seizing her hand and
stopping his walk.

They stood beneath a majestic elm; peace and
beauty brooded over the heaven and earth; there
was no living creature within hearing except the
little bird of which Sarah had spoken; she was
looking so beautiful in the soft light, and she
did not resent the almost harshness with which
Harry detained her.   Instead, she stood silent and
trembled.

"You know that I am not thinking of such
trifles," he continued.   "You know what is in my
thoughts, and you are trying to prevent my speaking.   But you *must* listen."

"Oh, no! I can not—not to night, Mr. Fletcher.
Do not say a word—I can not bear it. I would
not have you say what will cause me regret and
pain."

"You can not bear to hear me say that I love

you? Then, of course, it is because you can not
accept the love! Sarah, what do you mean, what
have you meant by your inexplicable conduct?
You must have known, for months, that my soul
was in your keeping."

His teeth were pressed into his lip as he tried to
regard her calmly; but try as his pride may
prompt him, when the one hope is at stake, a
man can not be indifferent.

"You have no right to question me. I have
not given you that encouragement which should
lead you to speak thus," exclaimed the young girl,
endeavoring to free her hand, while all the bad
elements in her nature arose imperiously, and she
raised a glance of fire to meet his own.

"You can say that with some truth, but not
with perfect candor. It is true that you have behaved willfully—at times kindly, at times coldly—
to me. But you have gone every day where I was
sure to meet you. You have been as gay, as
beautiful, as bewildering as it was possible for you
to be during those meetings. You have many
times aroused my deepest feelings by a thousand
womanly enchantments, and then—after proving

your power—shrank back into coldness when I would have spoken, if *that* is what you call not giving encouragement. But how could I decide that this was not merely girlish coquetry, that your heart was not mine, after all? You have received my constant attentions, and you have not received those of any other man. You shall not blame me that I love you: you shall feel the full weight of this result upon your own conscience. Now you shall tell me with your own lips whether you return my love or not. Oh, say that you do— that you have been trifling—that you are mine— *my* Sarah!" he exclaimed, with a sudden burst of passionate hope, as he saw her lids tremble with tears which dropped to her cheeks.

He was about to sustain with his arm the form that he would have given worlds to hold to his bosom now, as it seemed bending beneath some deep emotion.

" Would to heaven that I were yours!" she said in a low, sad voice. " Then I should be proud, be blessed, be happy. But I am not, and I can not be—never! It is utterly in vain to flatter you with a false expectation. I have done wrong, I have wronged you; and that is the bitterest drop in the cup. It may be a poor consolation for you to know that I am, at least, as miserable as you possibly can be; and I have brought all my unhappiness willfully upon my own head."

"No, Sarah, it is no consolation to me to feel that you suffer as I do at this moment. Neither do I believe it. A person capable of such feelings could never trifle with another. It is enough for you, in the pride of your youth and beauty, to bear with you the memory that you have broken a true heart."

He dropped those slender fingers from out of his cold hands and turned away. There was no anger in his tones, the keen anguish of their very coldness smote her heart like a sword.

With that strange impulsiveness which characterized her, she sprang to him and laid her hand upon his arm.

"Forgive me, Harry, or it will kill me. I cannot endure such language from you, who have been my friend always. If it will be any relief to your pain, know that I will never marry any other man. If I married any one it would be

you, and I would be your wife if I could make
you happy. But you have not my heart—it is
as grieved—as broken—more hopeless than your
own; it is not fit to mate with yours—it is an object of pity. Forgive me—and forget me, Harry."

She kissed him—a pure kiss of frièndliness and
sorrow—and while a tear which fell from her eyes
lay warm upon his hand, she fled away, leaving
him more in love, more in doubt than ever. He
stood where she left him, until she disappeared
up the lane which led toward her father's house,
and then he wandered into the solemn twilight
woods, the most wretched man, he thought, that
the stars ever came out to look down pitilessly
upon.

CHAPTER III.

"Within my breast there is no light,
But the cold light of stars;
I give the first watch of the night
To the red planet Mars."

LONGFELLOW.

"WHAT is the reason that Richard has not been to church for the past three weeks?" asked Mrs. Fletcher of her daughter Margaret.

They were sitting alone in the parlor at the old home; Margaret was spending the day with her mother, and had been playing old-fashioned airs for a long time on the piano, but was now engaged in making the button-holes in a shirt for her father, which the defective sight of the elder lady would not permit of her finishing.

"He does not like the minister," said the young wife; but her cheek colored a little, for she knew that this was not the sole reason; and she had been mortified by the fact that although Mr. Wilde had scrupulously kept his promise to attend church for six months, that the week the time mentioned had expired, he had, with some stubbornness, declined going again.

"He has n't the gift of an eloquent tongue, surely," replied the good mother; "but he preaches a safe and a sound doctrine; and it is much better to listen to him than not to go to meeting at all."

"Richard thinks that the parson is not as holy a man as he affects to be; that he is not so charitable and self-denying as he preaches. He says that he is obstinate and prejudiced, and Pharisaical—that he has got a very small, very selfish soul behind a very solemn face."

"Richard should be careful that he himself is not uncharitable. But if he is so strongly opposed to our minister, why does he not attend the Episcopalian services? We would not make any great objections, though we had rather have him with us. I feel uneasy about Richard's course, my dear."

"So do I," murmured Margaret, scarcely repressing a sigh. She would not tell her parent that she had urged her husband to attend the

4

Episcopalian church; and that he had good-naturedly but positively refused; giving as his reason, that he had so much law-business through the week, that he was obliged to take Sunday for general reading and refreshment.

"I hope I shall get him out with me again before many Sabbaths," she continued; "but he has been so busy lately that he is tired, and takes the holy day as a day of rest."

"Your father has been an industrious man the most of his days, Margaret, but he is never so tired that he has not a few hours to give to the worship of the Lord out of the whole week. And he has been a good husband to me. I hope we have not done wrong in marrying you to an unbeliever, my child.".

"So is Richard a good husband, mother," replied Margaret, quickly. "I love him more every hour of my life."

"Time will prove—time will prove," murmured the old lady. "It's a risk for a lamb of the fold to go wandering away from the flock in hopes to persuade a stray sheep. But I believe that you are a true Christian, my dear; and I can only counsel you to keep strict guard over your own conscience."

"You know what St. Paul says, mother: 'And the woman which hath an husband which believeth not, and if he be pleased to dwell with her, let her not leave him: for the unbelieving husband is sanctified by the wife, and the unbelieving wife is sanctified by the husband; for what knowest thou, O wife, whether thou shalt save thy husband?' I have faith that it will be given me to save Richard. He has such a noble nature—it only needs to be touched by Divine grace."

There was a sound as of tears in Margaret's voice, which showed how deeply in earnest she was —her mother could not find it in her heart to say any more on the subject.

A few moments afterward the young wife looked up from her sewing, and saw Richard coming across the lawn to take tea with the family, and accompany her home. She flung down her work, and bounding to the door to meet him, welcomed him as gladly as though they had been separated a week.

"It was lonely dining at home to-day. I am

afraid I did not do justice to Betty's dinner," Richard said, while she was untying the shawl from about his neck.

"And we could not half enjoy the turkey and cranberry-sauce because you were not here," she replied. "But you shall have some of it cold for supper. I have had such a pleasant day with mother; but the last two hours have been so long. Why did you not come sooner? it is five o'clock;" and then the husband laughed.

Mrs. Fletcher listened with a smile and sigh. Perhaps it was foolish of her to feel such forebodings about the future, as long as her son-in-law's actions were good and admirable; and she arose and met him with the same motherly kiss which she bestowed upon her own children.

When he took her hands, and held her away from him, and looked into her kindly eyes with his own dark, dancing ones, declaring that she was *almost* as young and handsome as Maggie, and that that was saying the most he could say, she yielded, like the rest, to the charm of his manner.

After half an hour's cheerful conversation they went to an early tea; for Richard wished to get back to town in time for an evening lecture at the court-house.

"Where is Harry?" asked he, as the meal was nearly finished. "He has not been in the village for two weeks, as I remember. Tell him we shall mark him out of our list."

"I saw him in the orchard as I came in," replied the father, "and he said he would be in presently."

"Something seems the matter with the lad. I am afraid he has taken a dislike to farm-life, or else his health is not going to be good. He is not the same boy that he was when you went away, Margaret. I think it is lonely for him out here, without any sister," remarked Mrs. Fletcher.

The young married couple looked at each other. *They* had the clew to his altered appearance; but, as he had kept his secret from his parents, they did not see fit to reveal it.

"If he would get a good wife, and bring her home here, it would make us all a little more lively, since Maggie has run away from us," said the old gentleman.

"I do not know who he would fancy, unless it was Sarah Irving," mused his wife.

5

"And she's quite too much of a fire-fly for any man, though she's pretty, and I like the gipsy. She's hardly the girl for Harry, though; and she has not joined the Church yet;" and Mr. Fletcher shook his head.

Richard smiled and colored slightly at the last objection, while the mother coughed as she asked him if he would have another cup of tea, and Margaret looked down upon her plate.

"She's a beautiful girl, for all that," said Richard; "and I hope she and Harry may sometime take it into their heads to get married."

"She's right smart, too; and can manage a house, when her mother is sick, as well as the best," added Mrs. Fletcher.

"Ah, well! I guess we had better wait until we see some signs of danger before we discuss the matter so seriously," laughed Margaret, as she arose from the table.

She was pained at the state of unhappiness which her brother was in, and she did not wish to fix attention upon it, so as to make it a source of any more speculation.

"Wrap up warm," was her mother's injunction,

as she was preparing for her long walk of two miles to the village.

"We will walk rapidly; that will be the best way to keep the cold off. Come, Maggie. Good-by, all."

The ground was frozen smooth, and a few flakes of snow fell slowly through the air, gray with the approaching evening. As they hurried down the lane by the orchard, they saw Harry, with his arms folded over the fence, and his head drooped upon them, gazing intently toward the house of the Irvings, just visible through a vista of trees at that spot.

"Why, Harry! you have not been to tea yet, and here you stand in the cold," spoke his sister, running up to him, and looking into his face with so much sadness and tenderness that he could not resent the sympathy her looks inferred. "Dear brother, I can not bear to see you so grave and pale. Come along with us to-night, will you not? Richard will be out, and I want you to sit with me."

"No—no! not to-night, Maggie. I had rather be alone."

She kissed his cheeks, and told him not to stand there any longer.

"Do come to town oftener. Cry 'Begone, dull care!' and whistle all melancholy down the wind," called out Richard to him, in a bluff, hearty voice, as his wife came back to him, and they passed along.

As they drew near to the residence of the Irvings, they saw that Sarah was out walking back and forth through the long front portico. It was a chilly night, and almost dark; there was already some snow gathering in the crevices around the house; but she wore no shawl or hood to protect her from the cold. The wind waved her black silk dress about her limbs, and tossed her hair, which was blacker than her dress. They could not see distinctly through the gathering gloom, but they thought that she looked thinner in face and form than when they met her last. She did not visit them now, except at long intervals, when she was quite certain that she should not meet Harry. They could not treat her coldly, despite of their sympathy with their brother; for they believed that she had not meant to wrong him, and they saw that for some mysterious reason she was unhappy. They could only love them both, and hope that sometime all would be well.

"How do you do, Sarah?" they called out, gayly, as they came opposite her in the road.

She lifted her head, answered faintly, "How do you do?" and re-commenced her lonely promenade.

"You will get sick, exposed to this bitter cold," cried out Margaret again.

"That would be a piece of good fortune," was the reply; and with this they left her to her thoughts.

CHAPTER IV.

"But man crouches and blushes,
  Absconds and conceals;
He creepeth and peepeth,
  He palters and steals."
                    RALPH WALDO EMERSON.

WE have said that Richard Wilde was ambitious, and that he was not quite content to settle
down in his native place. This might have been
the key to all his subsequent proceedings, although
it was not the motive the most prominently before his friends and the public.

The day after the one which ends the last
chapter, he told Margaret that he wished her to
attend a lecture with him in the evening. He
had been very deeply interested in the one of
the preceding night, and he wished her to go
and see if she would be as pleased as he had
been. The speaker was a stranger, and the subject was a religious one.

"A religious one!" Then the wife would be

glad to go, for the desire most fervent in her heart was that her husband might be influenced by the right, and withdrawn from the verge of that dangerous skepticism upon which he stood.

She went; and the man was a Mormon, and his object was to convert as many people as he could, and induce them to join the great caravan which was even then on its way from Missouri to the Great Salt Lake city, which had been chosen and laid out the previous summer. They had stopped, the most of them, for the winter, on the banks of the Missouri river, and would be glad to be joined by new friends and brethren before they began their journey in the spring.

Such arguments as might possibly deceive the unlearned and the very fanatical, were given with a kind of eager, rough eloquence, that was peculiarly the speaker's own; but not such reasoning as should have influenced an honest or intelligent mind. Margaret came away disgusted, and her husband came away a Mormon convert!

That was a very unpleasant night for the young wife. The two sat up until long past midnight discussing the subject which had suddenly be-

come of such vital importance to them. The
gentle nature of Margaret had never been so
thoroughly aroused in opposition to any matter
before; the glow burned upon her cheeks, and the
proud light flashed from her eyes as she heaped
indignant scorn upon the doctrines which had
been set forth. The one fearful vice which now
forms so prominent a feature of the Mormon institution had, at that time, been little discussed
by the public, and she was ignorant of its existence in that society. But the whole matter
wore to her such a look of farce and trickery
played off by a few leaders upon a foolish and
devoted people, that she was lost in astonishment
that her husband—Richard Wilde—whom she so
much admired and honored for his keen and
logical intellect—could be, for a moment, duped
or influenced.

"You are not in earnest, Richard!" she exclaimed,
bursting into tears, when he at length announced,
in answer to her plea, that he had resolved to
join the emigrants, and become one of the found-
ers of the future city.

"Now, Margaret," said her husband, drawing

her upon his knee, and caressing her; "you ought to be glad to hear that."

"*Glad* to leave my father and mother—my home—to go away into that wilderness!—and worse, to bring disgrace upon ourselves by *such* a religion! oh, Richard!"

"Have you not told me time and again, Maggie, that you would cheerfully sacrifice home, and country, and worldly prosperity, and all things, to see me a professor of the religion of Jesus Christ?"

"Yes, I have, Richard: and I would; but this is the mockery of false prophets—this is not the religion of Jesus Christ."

"Well, Margaret, my wife, I leave the decision of my future with you. I have always found it impossible to give my faith at all to the formal and repelling ceremonies which seem to me, in this community, to usurp the place of some real religion—if there be such a thing. And finding nothing here to fix my heart upon, I have fallen almost into a state of entire unbelief; doubts and perplexities have pressed upon me; and I have found my intellect warring with satire and phil-

osophy against my soul. But in this new institution I find something to attract and interest
me; my fancy, at least, if not my heart, is engaged; I think that I can see my way through
into a more satisfactory belief. It rests with you
whether you will encourage this, or throw me
back upon my old skepticism."

Poor Margaret! this was a new way of putting
the question to her. She felt that there was
something hollow in this speech, yet she could
not detect or expose it. And, perhaps, this was
the way in which her unwearied prayers for her
husband were to be answered; perhaps it was
only given her through sacrifice of much that
was dear to her, to be permitted to effect immortal good for him. And should she shrink
from the coveted test of her sincerity, now that
it had a shape different from what she expected?

That fathomless love, which lives in the heart
of a true woman for her husband and her God,
was stirred in her bosom to its deepest depths.
If it had been the martyrdom of herself, she
would not have shrunk, if convinced that her
husband's best interests demanded it. As it was,

the sacrifice was hardly less cruel—pride, old beliefs and associations, old loves and home had all to go.

"This has come suddenly upon me," she said, in a tremulous voice; "you have thrown such an awful weight upon my conscience, that, for the present, I am faint and confused. I will think of what you have said; and you know, dear Richard, that however I decide, it will be my love for you which prompts me."

The beautiful face, bathed in tears, sank upon his breast, and Richard, deeply moved by the unselfish affection which hallowed those sweet blue eyes, drew his wife more closely to his heart, and they sat in silence for several moments—a silence, the sweetest in the world, for it is not all silence when two hearts beat together as if they were one, and the bliss of living is made divine by being doubled. Even in the excited, unsettled state of their minds, they were happy.

Neither of them slept much that night. Richard had his own thoughts about the step he had resolved to take, and his wife was too deeply disturbed and grieved to rest; she passed the hours in a vain attempt to become reconciled to her new fortunes, and in silent supplication to the Source of all truth and wisdom to enlighten her as to what was her duty in this perilous case.

After daybreak she fell into a light slumber, and when her husband arose on his elbow and looked upon her beloved face, the flush of tears was yet upon her cheeks, and a slight contraction of the fair arched brow revealed to him the shadow which lurked in her usually happy dreams.

"I *am* asking her to resign a great deal for my sake," he mused. "She will give up all that is dear to her in the world to follow my fortunes. Dear Margaret! at least I will reward you with all the devotion which your heart can require."

"Do not look so sad, Margaret; do not, I beg of you," he said, as they sat at the breakfast-table, where the cup of coffee sat untasted by her plate.

"I was thinking of mother, Richard; and of how I should break the news to her."

"Are you not willing to 'leave father and

mother, and cleave unto your husband?' you, who are such a good Christian, Maggie?"

"If there is to be a choice between; but we were so happy all here together. I have hardly learned to do without my mother yet," said the young wife, with a faint smile. "And she—I am an only daughter, and I can not bear to leave her so desolate."

"It is the destiny of families to be scattered sooner or later, and when you became my wife you ought—"

"I know it—I know it! I do not hesitate a moment—that is, I would not if I were convinced that it was for your temporal or spiritual benefit that I should yield. But you will allow me some natural emotions of regret will you not, Richard?"

"Why, yes, my darling; and you must not think me so selfish as not to have dreaded this, too. It is hard, I know, and it pains me deeply. But I am acting now with reference to all our future, earthly and eternal, and I must not pause for trifles. Wherever we are, you will have me, Maggie, my love, my tenderness, my constant care for your happiness. We will be a thousand times
5

dearer to each other, even than now, when we have none but ourselves to cling to."

This appeal brought up from the depths of the bright eyes opposite him, a look of such glad devotion, that he knew his cause was gained. Nevertheless, when Mr. Wilde had gone out upon the business of the day, Margaret's heart was any thing but light. She felt as if she must fly to her mother for counsel; and yet she dreaded the hour when she should have to reveal a fact to her which was not only painful to the affections, but mortifying to their Puritan pride.

That day her husband brought home the Mormon missionary to dinner. She could scarcely treat him with ordinary politeness. He talked much and well, but she grew more disgusted with him every moment; not from any thing repelling in his appearance, but because of the influence he exerted over Richard. Their conversation was not so much upon the religious theories of his people as upon their future worldly prospects. The beauty and richness of the country which they were to appropriate—the means within themselves of amassing wealth—the ease with which men of talent and

education among them obtained eminence and position among the brethren—their prospects for becoming a mighty nation by themselves, and with
their own government—were some of the points
discussed.

"'First come—first served,' you know, Mr.
Wilde. *Now* is the time for a man of some fortune and more ability, like yourself, to make himself a name and fame, and secure to himself all the
exaltation of wealth and renown. Glorious prizes
are verily thrown at your feet, and if you do not
pick them up, the fault is your own."

Margaret sat listening, and weighing their words
in the correct balance of her pure mind. She felt
more discouraged than before ; a faint doubt of the
truthfulness of her husband's convictions, and the
possibility of some merely worldly motive influenc-
ing him, troubled her; yet she hardly knew which
was worst—that he really should be the disciple of
a false prophet, or that he should put on such a
guise for selfish purposes.

After dinner Richard went down town with the
missionary ; and Margaret, unable to bear the loneliness of the house, started to visit her mother. She

had a little black pony in the stable which she could saddle without assistance; and although it was a chilly winter day, she resolved to ride. The first mile, galloping along through the sharp, bright air, somewhat restored her spirits, when, all of a sudden, the thought rushed over her, that this familiar country, every acre of which was dear to her, must be deserted by her—these fields, these trees, this pleasant, winding road, even this precious jet-black steed, who had known no restraining hand but hers, were all to be changed for a strange, distasteful land;— her parents, her brothers, the old homestead, the ocean, whose grandeur had given a tinge of sublimity to her girlhood's dream, and which tossed restlessly but a few miles away—but most, her mother! The tears which ran rapidly down her cheeks so blinded her, that if the pony had not known its destination, he might have gone far astray.

"Now, for mercy's sake, child, what's the matter?" exclaimed Mrs. Fletcher, as Margaret came into the hall, her eyes red with weeping.

She only threw her arms about her mother and sobbed.

" In trouble so soon! What *has* happened, Maggie ?"

The young wife recovered herself with a quivering smile.

" I do believe it is only the first quarrel," spoke out the good mother, somewhat relieved. " Has Richard been cross, or denied you any thing, or neglected to kiss you when he went out of the house for an hour, baby ?"

" Oh, mother, it's a great deal worse than that. We are going out West early in the spring."

" Going out West, child ?"

" Yes ! into the far, far West; away off to Utah, mother."

" Utah ?" was the still incredulous question.

" Yes, mother. And, what is worst of all, we are going to the Great Salt Lake city; Richard's become a Mormon."

Mrs. Fletcher uttered a little scream. It was very seldom that she allowed her equanimity to be disturbed; but this was no trifling shock, and she sunk down into a chair, unable to give any other expression to her feelings.

" Don't look so sad, dear mother—don't; I feel

6

so badly already. And perhaps it's all for the best."

"All for the best! This comes from marrying an unbeliever. I do believe it's the judgment of heaven upon you. *My* daughter's husband join the Mormons! It's a disgrace—a burning disgrace. I know your father will feel it so. He, a deacon of the Church, and has always stood so high, to have a son-in-law a disciple of Jo Smith instead of Jesus Christ. This is what comes of being taken with fine talents, and fine looks, and fine education, instead of with goodness, and grace, and humility."

Perhaps this was the best thing the mother could have said to arrest Margaret's passionate weeping. If her friends were all to condemn Richard, she must defend him. So she dried her tears, and went over to his side of the argument. The objections she had so eloquently urged when talking with him the previous night, were left out of sight, and only his reasons and expectations given.

"It is your duty to stand by your husband, child, if you think he is right. He has already blinded your judgment. I know, my darling, that it is his

soul's salvation which you seek. But 'be not deceived; God is not mocked.'"

"Well, dearest mother, what else *can* I do?
Richard thinks he has found a rock to keep him
out of the ocean of skepticism: shall I push him off,
and leave him to struggle with its waters again?
You have often said that he had abundance of hard,
practical common sense. I trust greatly to that. I
think that when we arrive among this new people,
if his judgment is dissatisfied, that he will return.
He may lose a year or two of time, and some money
by the venture; but I shall stop to weigh nothing
in the scale against his spiritual welfare."

"'Ay, there's the rub.' If it only was for his
spiritual welfare," murmured Mrs. Fletcher, with a
deep sigh. "This is bad news to break to your
father."

"And how can I leave him, and leave you,
mother? Oh, I hope that Richard will change his
mind, and grow weary of Mormonism, and come
back again. Yet this may be the answer to my
prayers, mother!"

So it was that Margaret reconciled herself.

The saddest family group gathered around the

table that night which had been since the death of
a little sister years before. Mr. Fletcher did not
say as much as his wife had said, but he felt the
more deeply. He immediately detected in this sudden conversion some selfish, ambitious purpose,
which lay hidden from the unsuspicious eyes of
his wife and daughter

"Richard Wilde is too keen to be taken in the
trap of any such sham religion as that," he mused
in his heart. "A man that can argue as he can,
would never be duped by the doctrines of Jo
Smith. Something's at the bottom of this in the
shape of speculation. He'll make his fortune out
there, but I don't like the way. Honesty's the best
policy. Poor Maggie, I'm afraid for her."

The brothers were loud in their expressions of
disapprobation.

"I shall *hate* Richard, if he takes away my only
sister," muttered John, a sturdy boy of fourteen.
"And I thought him such a splendid fellow before."

Almost every body thought Richard Wilde a
"splendid fellow." That was the impression his
vivid wit and great tact in pleasing others, usually

left. He was so fond of being admired, that he did not despise the good opinion of a child, and generally he said and did something for all which delighted them. Yet many older heads who still thought him a " good fellow," mistrusted the depth of that goodness. The tendency to exaggerate, which made him brilliant, took from his sincerity. His impulses were not yet bad, only a little too selfish. He was generous to others, but most generous to himself. He, himself, having not yet been tried in any great ordeal, thought himself a good, perhaps a splendid fellow, and that his lily-flower Margaret showed great discretion in loving him as she did. He adored her with a kind of passion and unrest which did not promise as well for duration as for strength ; but of this the pure and single-hearted woman never dreamed.

Harry, like his father, did not say much. He had seemed less cheerful even, when he first came in, than when she had met him the day previous. After hearing the exciting news, he fell into a reverie from which he aroused himself, looking more happy than he had done for a long time.

" I do believe Harry is glad that we are going,"
said Margaret.

"I am glad; I think it will be a good thing
for Richard."

This decision filled the family with surprise.
Margaret was comforted by it, for she placed confidence in her brother. Far from her remotest
thought was any idea of the true cause which
influenced his opinion.

As they always gave her an early tea, the young
wife hoped to reach home in time to preside over
his cup for her husband; she did not like him to
eat in solitude.

So telling them all that she would see them
soon again on the now-engrossing subject of her
visit, she sprang upon her pony and bounded away.

As she passed the Irvings', she saw Sarah, with
bonnet and cloak, waiting at the gate.

" Check the speed of your fiery steed, for I want
your company into town," she said, as she came
forth to meet her.

"Then you must get up behind, for I am in
haste, and pony would n't like to measure his
steps with your little feet."

"If you were an old-fashioned cavalier, there would be something worth while in mounting the same steed and flying away into the regions of sunset, with the sounds of hot pursuit dying in the distance," laughed Sarah, as she sprang up, and the little pony cantered away, looking rather overloaded.

"You are too romantic for this common-place era, Sarah; you ought to have been born in the days of troubadours; those bright, proud eyes of yours would have brought plenty of them to sigh beneath your window. You must marry, and settle down soberly, like me."

"What do I care for these eyes of mine, since their arrows could not bring down the game I wanted? Do not talk to me about settling down soberly. I never did any thing as other people do; and I have a presentiment that I shall not marry as other people marry. By the way, I heard a very strange rumor this afternoon."

"That we were going west?"

" Yes."

"Well, I fear that it is too true."

There was a long silence; at length Sarah spoke

in a low voice, full of meaning, which startled her friend.

"Do you know that the Mormons believe in polygamy, Margaret?"

She felt the heart around which her arm was thrown give a sudden leap, but it grew composed again.

"No," was the reply; "and I do not believe it."

"Well, it is so."

"If Richard knew that he would not go near them," said the wife, at length; "he would be too much shocked. I think you must be mistaken: there are so many reports."

Sarah did not repeat the charge, and Margaret went on to tell her about the lecture and the missionary, etc., until they reached her home.

"I am just in the mood for riding a little further," said Sara, as the other dismounted, "and if you do not object to loaning your horse for a half hour, I will ride on."

"I would loan you any thing I possessed, except the heart of my husband. But is it not too cold to ride so near night?"

"Not too cold for me: I love it."

She sprang into the seat, and waving her hand with a grace which none but herself might equal, she touched the fiery little pony with the whip, and away they flew down a cross-street leading out into a road which ran down to the sea. There was no wind, but the air was sharp, and the sun was low. Her cheeks were crimson with the cold; her hood fell back, and her glossy black hair floated around her face in disorderly curls. If James could have seen her in that declin-ing winter light, he would thereafter have written eternally about one young horsewoman riding down upon the beach, instead of two horsemen riding over a hill—if indeed he did not mistake her for an apparition, and write about a spirit upon a bewitched steed. Before he would have time to rub his eyes and convince himself, she would have been out of sight as by magic, so madly she hurried her swift little horse along the path.

It was half an hour's ride to the ocean, and although she had only asked to be gone that length of time, when she came in sight of those eternal waves, the same spirit which had prompted the ride, impelled her on to the shore. Ah, how

cold it was there, and the sun was sinking behind
her. But the moon was rising before her. Out
of that bed of silvery ripples in the dim distance
she came up, and hung cold and bright over a
glittering waste.

Sarah Irving rode to and fro along the gravelly
beach. There were none in that lonely spot to
wonder at her mood, only the poor pony whom
she gave not time to breathe, as she urged him
back and forth. Her eyes, growing darker and
more intense, looked over the boundless waters.
As moonlight took the place of day, she too began
to look pallid and wan; the ocean had on a ghostly
splendor which was reflected in her face. The
waves rolled in upon the beach, expiring with a
prolonged cry. By-and-by she too began to cry
out in a long, low voice, "Oh, no, I can not, I can
not!" she cried, and then the next moment, "but
I will—I must!" No other human being could
have rightly guessed the secret of the struggle in
her swelling breast. It heaved with sighs like
the infinite bosom of the sea before her.

"Oh, sea!" she sobbed at last, turning her
horse's head, and facing it, "we must have some-

thing in common, so strangely do you sympathize with my words. But you are more or less than human. I, alas, am human; in my breast is the war of passion against principle: you know not the awful strife. Yet your voice is sadder, your sighs more mighty than mine. Can you feel more than I do? Have you a grief? do you know mortal or immortal pain like mine?"

The tide was coming in; even as she ceased speaking, the waves, crested with glittering foam, broke around her horse's feet, who plunged and shivered beneath her restraining hand; she sat erect and held him subdued.

"I knew that you returned my love," she continued; "and here you are creeping close to me at the sound of my voice, to assure me of your good understanding with me. We are friends. Are we not both wild, and fascinating, and sad, and unrestrainable? You have many lovers, ocean! and so have I; but I have not the one whom alone of all I sought. You toss ships, and treasures, and men into destruction to prove your power; why should not I toss one poor, feeble heart aside, to prove mine?"

Perhaps she waited for an answer to her hard question, forgetful, in the whirl of her excited mind, that the friendship of the sea was not to be trusted; again the breakers rolled in; and this time they swept her away. They hurled her off her horse, whose frightened scream she heard as the cold waves deluged him. They drove the blinding mist into her eyes; they seized upon her breath; they chilled her heart, and she knew no more of what they did with her.

The sea was not very cruel, after all. It would do by her as she would do by others: if she would toss a human heart aside as mad, it would toss her aside; yet not quite hopelessly. When it had played with her a moment, it threw her chilled and senseless upon the pitiless shore, where she must have very soon perished, had not a horseman, as by providence, come riding down that way.

It was Harry Fletcher, who had followed his sister into town to talk with Richard about the news, and had been sent by her in search of the long-absent girl who had ridden off alone toward the ocean. He threw himself beside her, and drag-

ged her away from danger; he took her head upon
his bosom, and chafed her hands, and kissed her
lips; it was in vain to try to resuscitate her there,
and her wet garments were freezing around her.
He flung her light form over his horse's neck,
sprang into the saddle, and rode to the first farm-
house.

Poor Jenny, Margaret's beautiful black pony,
was not thought of in that moment; the waves
did not treat her as kindly as they did the mistress who compelled her into danger—she drifted
out, and went down to darkness and death.

The people who lived at the farm-house had a
large fire and a bed in the sitting-room. They had
had cases of drowning to attend to before this one,
and with skill and kindness they soon revived the
sufferer. The woman put dry garments upon her,
covered her in the bed, and gave her a little wine.
Harry was admitted to see her lying pale and beautiful upon the pillow, to hear her whisper, " I
thank you," to him, as her preserver—for although
Sarah was not happy, she was young, and not
really quite ready to die—to meet the glance of
her sad eyes beaming almost tenderly upon him,

6

and then he rode away after Margaret to come and
stay the night with her.

When he returned with his sister, they found her
doing very well; there was a faint color in her
cheeks borrowed from the heat of the fire which
blazed opposite; she looked so subdued and gentle
that she was hardly like the same Sarah who had
left her home two hours before. Her hair, from
which the salt sea was drying, had parted into a
thousand little shining strands, indescribably beautiful. Harry, now that the fright was over, was
completely overcome; his overstretched nerves relaxed; as he sat by the bed the tears welled quietly
from his eyes, and were wiped away. The people
were all out of the room, and Margaret went too
for something which the invalid needed.

"You need not weep any more," said the young
girl in a faint voice, reaching out her hand across
the bed to him; "you shall have the life which
you have saved."

He gazed at her an instant as if afraid that he
mistook.

"If you dare take so wild a creature, I will be
yours."

The half smile and blush assured him that he had heard aright; and he bowed his lips to that hand which had been given him, in a thrill of joy too sudden for words.

CHAPTER V.

"The breath of the morning is with her,
   Wherever my darling goes.

"What if, with her sunny hair,
   And smile as sunny as sweet,
She meant to weave me a snare
   Of some coquettish deceit?"

TENNYSON'S "MAUD."

SARAH IRVING had neither father nor mother.
She inherited a few thousand dollars, over which
she now, being of age, held entire control, and
lived with an uncle and aunt who were childless.
They loved her very tenderly, and had indulged
her too much for the true good of so wayward a
spirit. After losing her parents, and when between eight and twelve years of age, she had
visited amid her friends and relations, her home
being unsettled; and as she was beautiful, winning, and heiress to some wealth, she was every-
where petted and caressed. The strong will of
her wild but interesting nature grew unchecked;
when she finally found a permanent resting-place

at her Uncle Irving's. They were afraid of even
the appearance of unkindness to the orphan, and
allowed her to grow just as her own character
inclined itself.

All the wildness about her might have been
trained into exquisite proportions, but she came
up like the forest vine. All owned the charm
of her very willfulness, while few foresaw that it
would ever bring her any trouble.

All that there was unusual about her was very
bewitching. Her laughter and her frown had beauty in them; her gracefulness knew no rules; she
herself made the laws which governed her dress
and her manners. If, sometimes, she was angry,
it was only a flash of summer lightning. breaking out from her dark eyes, and revealing more
clearly her warm and glorious beauty. If she
took offense without reason, she was as quick as
the humblest child to implore pardon for her mis-
deeds.

So here she was in her nineteenth year, and no
persons but the envious had ever found serious
fault with her, until the next morning after her
accident, when her aunt and uncle heard of her

7

last night's peril. They had supposed her safe at
Mr. Wilde's, until the news arrived, by way of
Harry, the next day; and then their fright and
anxiety convinced them, for the first time, that
their niece was altogether too careless, and too full
of wild freaks to be trusted; and they gave the
poor child a lecture, meant to be very severe,
when they arrived at the cottage where she was
waiting to be taken home.

The husky voice in which her uncle scolded, and
the kiss with which her aunt was finally obliged to
turn suspicion from a tell-tale tear, showed Sarah
that they were not half so offended with her as she
deserved. She got comfortably home, and there
was nothing then to cry about but the loss of the
pony. Margaret shed many tears for him, and
Sarah accused herself vehemently for his loss.

Harry could not grieve even for poor Jenny.
He thought his happiness cheaply purchased by
her life. If he had been as cool and calm in his
love-matters as in his business affairs, his good
sense would have taught him to have feared the
stability of words spoken under such circumstances.
Gratitude is not love; and it remained to show

whether even that sentiment would diminish or
increase. He did not stop to think; his being was
absorbed in feeling; his mental faculties were
buried in a delicious stupor, while his heart held
high revel.

That evening he went to see Sarah. He found
her sitting in a large arm-chair before the fire,
a crimson shawl wrapped about her, and the hair
brushed back plainly from her somewhat pale fore-
head, and falling in clusters of curls around her
shoulders. She received him very quietly, yet
very pleasantly; he had never seen her when she
appeared so perfectly contented, and to be enjoying
such sweet repose; every trace of restlessness had
gone from her voice and manner. It was the calm
after the tempest; the peace of exhaustion; the girl
felt as if her destiny had been decided for her, and
she was too weary to struggle with it any longer—
she would take it as it came, and be glad that
circumstances had taken the trouble of any further
doubt away from her.

If a dream had flitted across his brain during
the day, that a promise made under such exciting
impulses should not be relied upon, he forgot it

now, as he gazed and gazed upon that serene countenance with the intensity of hope and passion. Her aunt had said, as she retired to her own sitting-room, that Sarah must go to bed early; and Harry, fearful of fatiguing her, staid but a little while, and made no reference to the great event of the previous evening. But when he arose to go, he bent over her, and pressed his first kiss upon her lips; then he looked into her face with a lover's boldness, to see how she received it. Her eyes were cast down, but she neither smiled nor frowned. Oh, how he yearned to have her look up and give him one radiant glance in answer to the love which was beaming from his gaze—one of ·her sweet, swift glances, only it should be touched with a new beauty of timidity and affection; but those eyes were still modestly downcast, so he said "good-night," softly, and went out from her presence.

It was a great comfort to Margaret to hear of the engagement of Sarah to her brother. She was rejoiced not only that their happiness seemed now secured, but she felt much more contented about leaving her mother, since a new daughter was going into the family, whose high spirits would keep loneliness from haunting the old homestead, and whose merry fingers and sweet voice would fill the parlor with the old, beloved melodies.

The holidays came and were spent in the usual round of feasting and gayeties, the cheerfulness becoming to the season being shaded a little by the thought that it was the last time for many years that Margaret would grace the family circle Richard said that just as soon as the great tide of emigration setting westward made the journey back less difficult, that his wife should return and stay as long as she wished; but it would be a long time before they could hope for such a state of civilization, and in the mean time, what might not happen? Who, of all these dear ones, would be missed from the group, when she returned? Would her mother not probably be taken away before that? What loss might not sickness and accident bring? Such questions were continually stirring in Margaret's heart, and dimming her eyes with tears in the midst of the brightest hours.

After New Year's they were all very busy aiding

in the preparation for the long and wearisome journey. Richard had his business to settle up, and Margaret the providing of such comforts as it was possible to take with them. Sarah sewed for her many an hour, and Mrs. Fletcher's most abiding thought was—" What more can I do for them? what else can I add to their store of necessaries ?"

The young couple had possessed a large circle of friends and admirers; but the tide of popular feeling was now against them, and there were but few who expressed their good-will either by cheering words or tokens of affection.

Richard's own father was very bitter; the minister was bitterer still. He called upon Mrs. Wilde, when he first heard of their intention, to know if it was possible that she, a member of his church, could cast such discredit upon her profession, as to consent, for any reason, to accompany her husband into the midst of a wicked and false people.

Margaret wept a good deal during his visit, and expressed her own regret at the step, but said firmly that where Richard went she must go, and expressed her hope that this delusion of his might result in the conversion of his soul to the true religion in the course of time.

The pastor represented the enormities and idol-atries of the Mormons in indignant terms, and left his lamb of the fold feeling very lost, unsettled, and unhappy. Richard, in turn, had an equally warm and indignant defense to set up: he dwelt upon the persecutions to which a homeless and peaceful people had been subjected; called for proof that there was any thing evil in their habits or belief; commended their wisdom and prudence, and their wonderful patience, perseverance and in-dustry. He painted their future success and pros-perity in, almost too glowing terms; for Margaret apprehended that his mind was more captivated by the projected splendor of their worldly enterprises, than by their religion.

She had nothing to do, however, but to sub-mit, to pray more fervently, and to trust, with a woman's faith, that all would be well.

As for Harry, as the weeks flew by he was not quite so happy as he had expected to be. Sarah had gone back into her old capricious moods; and try to be satisfied as he might, he could not shake off a feeling of discontent at her conduct. Sometimes she was wrapped away out of his sight in a cloak of cold reserve; again she was sad, and could give no explanation of her gloom; then she put on a bewildering, tantalizing gayety; occasionally she gave him a playful caress or a thrilling glance, but never did he find her in that subdued, tender and loving mood for which he longed.

"She does not love me, and she will never make me happy—why do I not resign her at once?" he asked himself again and again, and always the answer was—"I can not give her up; she is only wayward, a wild bird that refuses to be tamed, yet ah! so beautiful!"

And at the vision of her beauty the resolution to prove himself wise and proud melted into air.

One evening he sat with her and others in her uncle's parlor. She was in one of her unapproachable and queenly guises, not petulant, but cold. She sat near the lamp, and made it an excuse to be very busy with her crocheting of a purse for him, that she need talk but little. He asked to hold the little ball of blue silk, but she put it in her pocket; he essayed to make her drop a stitch and she received his pleasantry very seriously.

At last he gave up the hope of interesting her and sat gazing rather sullenly upon her bright, impassive face, with its downcast eyes fixed upon her work. Suddenly a step and voice were heard in the hall; the blood rushed into Sarah's cheeks; her hand trembled so that she dropped more than one stitch; the full blaze of the lamp shone upon her, and Harry could see how her heart beat rapidly beneath its bodice. She was aware that she had betrayed agitation, and she turned her chair nervously so as to shade her face.

It was only Richard Wilde who entered, and presently the young girl was calm again; but her lover was not; he it was who was now silent and reserved, yet who noted with a jealous eye how soft and rich a tone her voice took on unconsciously as she answered the new comer, how the flush lingered on her cheek, and how she stole glances at his married brother which he would have periled his soul to win. In vain she now became condescending and social to him, striving to cover past haughtiness with present humility; gloom was upon his brow and the agony of mistrust in his heart. Harry might have been mistaken in his fierce sus-picion; he was a jealous lover, and

> " Trifles light as air
> Are, to the jealous, confirmation strong
> As proofs of holy writ."

CHAPTER VI.

"And ever in soft dreams
Of future love and peace sweet converse lapt
Our willing fancies, till the pallid beams
Of the last watchfire fell, and darkness wrapt
The waves, and each bright chain of floating fire was snapt

"And till we came even to the city's wall,
And the great gate, then, none knew whence or why
Disquiet on the multitude did fall."
SHELLEY.

THE twentieth day of March had arrived—the day set for the departure of Richard and Margaret from the home of their youth for a far, uncivilized land. They were to go to New York, and there join a company who were bound for the same goal, proceed from there to St. Louis by railroad, take a boat up the Missouri, buying horses and wagons at the latter city to use in passing the vast plains and discouraging mountains which lay between the furthermost-bound boat and their remote destination.

A weeping group was gathered about the youthful adventurers. Margaret summoned all her res-

olution when the carriage, which was to convey
them to the dépôt, came to the door. One by one
her friends embraced her, and their tears fell hot
upon her cheeks. She would not give way to the
sobs which choke-l her when her father and mother
took her in their arms, for fear of adding to their
already too burdensome grief. Last of all came
Sarah to say good-by. She had been laughing and
jesting all the morning, as it seemed, with a brave
endeavor to keep up the spirits of the rest of the
party; but as she gave her hand to Richard, and
he kissed her with tear-blinded eyes as he had the
rest of his friends, she turned very pale. Giving
her hand from his grasp to that of Margaret, she
tried to say her farewell, but her lips quivered
without any sound, and she fell fainting into her
arms. Here was an event which added to their
already excited feelings; but the carriage could not
wait. Margaret kissed the white cheek of her
childhood's companion, and amid repressed sobs
of grief, was led out and lifted into the vehicle.

Their first half-day's ride was gloomy enough.
Margaret had her vail over her face to conceal the
tears which flowed silently but plentifully. There

was something exhilarating in the swift motion of the cars, and her unrestrained weeping had " eased her heart," so that, at last, by the persuasions of Richard, she lifted her vail, and allowed herself to be diverted by the variety of scenes through which they impetuously swept.

In New York they had a day or two of sight-seeing, the rest of the company not being quite ready for their journey. Her husband was so full of hope and animation, that Margaret would have been tolerably content were it not for the thought of those she was leaving behind. She had traveled but little—a trip to Niagara with her father being almost the extent of her experiences—so that all things had the charm of novelty.

Their company was made up of the superior class of emigrants—men like Richard, who were of some fortune and education, and who, perhaps, like him, had some other than religious motives in embarking their all in such a venture—with their families, women following their husbands as Ruth did Naomi, and a few children who knew but little except of the pleasures of continual change.

They were weary enough of their long ride when

7

they reached St. Louis; here they had a day or two
in which to rest, while procuring stores for their
journey, cattle, wagons and provisions, and waiting for a boat.

The spring rain had swelled the river, so that
their boat panted and puffed along quite steadily.
They were ten days in reaching Council Bluffs,
where they were to begin the most tedious part of
their wanderings.

Those ten days were really enjoyed by Margaret.
She had now become somewhat acquainted with
her fellow-passengers, with all of whom she was
rendered a favorite by her personal beauty and
sweetness of disposition. Many of them she liked
in return. They had various kinds of amusements
to beguile their time going on in the cabin; but as
the weather was quite warm and dry, it was her
chief enjoyment to sit out on deck with Richard,
marking the scenery through which they passed,
and talking over the future and the past. Not
even in the days of their betrothal had he been at
more pains to make himself agreeable to her. He
seemed to dread lest home-sickness should take
possession of her, and to avert that calamity he was

more lover-like than ever. As they passed the Bluffs, which rose in beautiful terraces, now close to the shore, and now sweeping further back into the country, he would point out every new charm, and talk with a winning eloquence about the wild, free, beautiful life they would live in that far away new world, that wonderful Atlantis, where all of nature's magnificence would be theirs, and wealth and honor had only to be sought and found.

The conventionalities, the cold-hearted formalities of civilized barbarism should not fetter them there. It is true that they would dwell in a city, but a city unlike any other that ever was built—a city of sisters and brothers living in peace and delight. They would be free to worship in the grandest temples of nature, to love the beautiful, to grow out of the harshness and conventionality of old ceremonies each into his own individuality. Their natures would expand like the glorious prairies around them, and their unfettered hearts would expand with the worship of all things pure, and truthful, and free, and thus they would ever become capable of a more perfect love toward one another. As their spiritual being grew in beauty toward the Above, their union would become still more what the angels would contemplate with pleasure, so that the ever-increasing fairness of their pathway through life would lead them, at length, both to a still more lovely life in another world.

These were a few of the anticipations which he poured into her fascinated ear as they sat alone on the deck, oftentimes in the mystic moonlight, which gave all their surroundings a weird and softened look, while her little hand nestled itself in his, and he rounded all his most eloquent periods with a kiss upon her smiling mouth. How could she choose but take him at his word, and believe that they were really just about entering a new Atlantis, the most beautiful the world ever dreamed of? At least, whether it were a desert or a paradise, she was with her husband, and he loved her, and would love her yet more and more.

Arrived at Council Bluffs the party put themselves in marching order. They joined another company who had come from St. Louis in wagons, and, in all, numbered a hundred fighting men, who were all well armed, and half as many women and children. There was quite an array, and as the weather was fine and provisions ample, the emigrants were in fine spirits.

A slight cloud came over them, though, the first day, as they reached the little village, a few miles beyond Council Bluffs, where the Mormons had wintered, a large body of them, the season before. They had extemporized this village for their winter quarters; cold, famine, and disease had made sad havoc with their numbers, and more than a hundred new-made graves met the startled eyes of their brethren who followed after/ This unfortunate company of saints, when they left, but a few weeks previous, this, their unhappy stopping-place, shook the dust from off their feet, and cursed it in sorrow and bitterness of heart

The memory of the rest of that long and perilous pilgrimage became afterward like a fever-dream to Margaret; it haunted her like something she had endured, and yet which had no reality. During its progress she thought often of that vivid picture in "Alton Locke's" wonderful fever-vision. She repeated it to her husband; and as it is an altogether more true and sublime history of her journeying than we can give, we quote it:

8

"The noise of wheels crushing slowly through meadows of tall marigolds and asters, orchises and fragrant lilies. * * * So I slept, and woke, and slept again, day after day, week after week, in the lazy bullock-wagon, among herds of gray cattle guarded by huge, lop-eared mastiffs; among shaggy, white horses, heavy-horned sheep, and silky goats; among tall, bare-limbed men, with stone axes on their shoulders and horn bows at their backs. Westward, through the boundless steppes, whither or why we knew not, but that the All-Father had sent us forth. And behind us, the rosy snow-peaks died into ghastly gray, lower and lower as every evening came; and before us the plains spread infinite, with gleaming salt-lakes, and ever fresh tribes of gaudy flowers. Behind us, dark lines of living beings streamed down the mountain slopes; around us, dark lines crawled along the plains—all westward—westward ever. The tribes of the Holy Mountain poured out like water to replenish the earth and subdue it—love-streams from the creator of that great soul-volcano—Titan babes, dumb angels of God, bearing with them, in their unconscious pregnancy, the law, the freedom, the science, the poetry, the Christianity of Europe and the world.

"Westward ever—who could stand against us? We met the wild asses on the steppe, and tamed them, and made them our slaves. We slew the bison-herds, and swam broad rivers on their skins. The Python-snake lay across our path ; the wolves and the wild dogs snarled at us out of their coverts ; we slew them, and went on. The forests rose in black, tangled barriers ; we hewed our way through them, and went on. Strange giant tribes met us, and eagle-visaged hordes, fierce and foolish ; we smote them, hip and thigh, and went on—westward ever. Days and weeks rolled on, and our wheels rolled on with them."

So to Margaret's excited imagination seemed their long, long wanderings. She saw great prairies all in a whirl and splendor of flame ; broad, nameless rivers glittered in the sunlight ; she breathed the aroma of unknown flowers ; she heard the scream of the panther and the yell of the wild Indian ; she saw hills standing up against the sky, which they were to wearily climb ; she trembled at times with fear, and again she thrilled with speechless pleasure

as she looked abroad over lands of wonderful magnificence.

They left more than one new grave to its awful
solitude in the wilderness; and they welcomed two
or three infant souls, born in sorrow and discomfort,
to a place in their never-resting company. More
than once they thirsted for water, and were mocked
by glittering springs and pools of salt and bitter
waters; again, they feasted upon delicious berries
gathered at morning from the dewy plains; and so
with joy and pain they traveled on, till they found
an abiding-place in the eager, hospitable heart of
the Great City of the Saints.

CHAPTER VII.

"The mother, with her dewy eye,
Is dearer than the blushing bride
Who stood, three happy years gone by,
In beauty by my side."
BURLEIGH.

FOR a couple of months after their arrival, the Wildes, like many others, lived in a tent or canvas house. It was glorious autumn weather; the world around them had on a gorgeous appareling of purple mist, and flowery prairies, and many-hued foliage, such as they had never seen in their chilly, New England home ; and Margaret, for a time, was all enthusiasm. Her novel mode of life had a thousand charms for her poetical nature, which had found but little at home to stimulate, it, except the ocean, ever grand, ever unequaled, and whose green or purple waves she loved to fancy in the soft swell of the grassy plains lying beneath her gaze. It was a luxury to sit in her tent-door and feel the delicious air blowing about her, sweet with the breath of a million dying blossoms; and a still greater luxury to mount the Indian pony which Richard had presented her, and ride away by his side into the sublime solitudes which surrounded the city.

Bitter drops soon began to distill into her cup of sweets. Her day-dreams were broken in upon constantly by uncongenial companions. The women of Utah were talkative and inquisitive—more than women usually are, for the simple reason that their homes were not happy—and they did not believe in any of their number setting themselves up to be unsocial or exclusive. They were disposed to show Margaret more attention than she cared to reciprocate. She was very much disappointed in the character of the community generally. She was a stout republican, and yet she felt it impossible to fraternize with some who claimed her friendship.

The city itself was busy, prosperous, neat and pleasant; and Richard was full of animation and ambition; but Margaret grew all the time less satisfied. She began to get glimpses of the true state of religion and domestic morals amid the people. She could hardly tolerate their religious ceremonies, but attended them in obedience to the wishes of her husband. Her pure nature was inexpressibly shock-ed by those other principles which she dreaded, and yet was compelled to believe were rife amid the community. Richard glossed the matter over for a while to her, but her female friends were continually revealing facts to her, and endeavoring to elicit her sentiments. She gave them no room to doubt of her displeasure and detestation. The severity of her rebuke was more than they could bear, and Richard was soon given to understand that his wife must use more discretion—that it was not becoming for a stranger in their midst to inveigh against ex-isting institutions.

Richard's desires that she should keep her own counsels, were very earnestly expressed. He was ambitious; he wished to make a fortune; but most he aspired to gain influence over his fellow-men. This, by means of his tact and brilliant talents, he was rapidly acquiring, and he could not be thwart-ed in his aims by having a prejudice gotten up against his beautiful wife. He wished her to con-ciliate—to use her fine powers of pleasing, as he did his own, for selfish purposes. But this he dared not ask of her; in truth, he was not yet so selfish in his love of power, that he wished to see *his wife* any less modest, truthful, gentle, and pure than she was.

When talking with her, he condemned, as heartily as she could wish, the sin which threatened to undermine their social foundations, but he made her promise silence.

Margaret was almost sorry when their little adobe house was finished—the tent was so novel and charming; but a cold breath of wind sweeping in through the canvas, proclaimed the approach of winter, and the comforts of a more substantial dwelling.

"It is not equal to the home we left," she said with a sigh, when the few articles of plain furniture were arranged in the four small rooms which completed the cottage. "Oh, for my beloved piano, and our books, Richard!"

"Wait just a few years until we have our railroad built, darling; then you shall have a piano, and every thing else that your heart can imagine. This is but a temporary home. I am going to be a rich man, Maggie, a very rich man;

and you are to reign as a kind of queen over this new Atlantis."

"Ah, Richard, I have no ambition of that kind; I only dread lest your glowing schemes lead you unconsciously into selfishness. I only fear that your heart, which is now all mine, will be divided between me and the idols of your earthly ambition. For the world with all its splendor, I would not have you lose your singleness of heart, your pure tastes, your love of the beautiful, your devotion to me," she added with a blushing smile, though the tears were in her eyes, so earnestly she spoke.

She put her arms about his neck, and leaned her head in her child-like manner against his breast.

"The touch of this beautiful head upon my bosom is worth more than all my hopes of worldly success to me," he said, in his most deep and tender tone. "Never—never shall I do any thing which shall prevent it from reposing thus confidingly upon my heart, my wife Margaret."

"My wife Margaret!" the musical, impassioned tone his voice assumed in breathing her name, thrilled her heart with the sweetest happiness. Her new home grew all perfection to her then.

It was invested with the one glory which alone
can gild with true splendor either palace or cottage; the one radiance whose beauty no jewels
can emulate; the one sunlight which makes summer in the dreariest climate.

"I am content with your love; and would be anywhere," she said, after a moment of blissful silence.

"And a loving husband may atone for the want
of a piano?" he asked, playfully.

"Yes; that is, if he will sing for me the songs he
used to sing in the moonlight nights at home. His
voice is sweeter to me than any instrument."

"For that piece of flattery, then, I will repay you
with your old favorite—let me see, which one?"

"I can wait a little while," said Margaret, laughing. "Moonlight airs will not sound accordant
before tea. Look! the table is spread, and we will
partake of our first feast in the new house; and it
will really be a feast, for a neighbor brought us
this delicious wild-honey to-day, and here are your
favorite cakes. We have coffee, too, made of
barley, which, with rich cream, is a drink not to be
scorned. We will have to drink it altogether,
hereafter, for I have given away all the tea we

brought with us to the old ladies of my acquaintance, who are not used to being deprived of it, and
who really need it. That was right, was n't it
dear? for you care but little about tea, and we are
young, and can do without."

"It was just like you, Maggie, and so I can not
say that I have any fault to find," was the affectionate reply; "though I think you had better have
saved one paper for yourself; you may need it by-
and-by."

"Not so much as they. How do you like bar-
ley-coffee?"

"It's as good as Mocha for me. This wild-
honey is one of the sweets of barbarism, is n't it?"

"Say rather of nature. And I think it all the
more delicious when I remember that it was gathered from prairie-flowers by bees, yellow-belted,
striped, and tattooed like Indian furies, coming
down in tiny hordes upon the frightened blossoms,
with spears all poised, to rifle them of their precious
stores. There is something romantic about our
repast, not unfit to be associated with poetry, re-
minding me of the feasting of Adam and Eve."

"That kind of poetic feeling is associated with

almost all that I do," replied Richard. "There is a charm—the charm of wildness, and freedom from old customs—about every thing; as if, in this far-away west, we were indeed living in the beginning of creation, or, at least, in another, newer world. There is nothing to trammel my energies, no precedent which I must follow, every thing is free, and great, and boundless, and my spirit swells to a kindred greatness."

"If it only were not for the people, Richard, I should think that our dreams might be realized. But any amount of self-deception can not hide the fact that, instead of escaping the evils and stains of society, we have riveted around us those of a more degrading kind. Instead of the reserve and coldness of New England civilization, we have the interference and curiosity of ignorance and prejudice. If we were living in the midst of a few choice people, such as we would have chosen for ourselves, we should indeed believe the Atlantis was found."

"What do you think," said Richard, after a pause, " was proposed, to me, to-day, by one of the leading elders?"

Margaret drew in her breath, and said she could not guess.

"Nothing less than that, as my new house was now finished, and had four good rooms, and as I promised fair to be a man of influence, he thought it best for me to set a good example by taking another wife."

The young husband laughed merrily at the indignant and breathless scorn of his beautiful companion.

"How did he dare to insult you so grossly?" she asked, when she had recovered somewhat from her astonishment.

"Do you suppose he thought it an insult, darling?"

"But I am sure you showed him that you considered it so."

'Well, I told him that I was a good Mormon, but that I must have the privilege of managing my domestic affairs as I pleased; that I loved the wife I had very dearly, and could not think of taking another as long as that was the case."

"I presume some envious woman who begrudged me my happiness was at the bottom of the suggestion," said Margaret.

8

"Or, perhaps, some woman who has become en-amored of my beauty," said Richard, laughing at his own vanity.

"I should not wonder," answered the wife, look-ing up into his handsome face with a proud smile. "As if she thought my Richard was to be won!"

"They little dream of what true love is, Maggie, or true happiness, either. Strange! that people will thus wreck their own best interests, and involve themselves in all kinds of intricate, miry laby-rinths, chasing after an *ignis fatuus*, when the star of peace burns brightly at home. But since we are among them we must take the good and leave the evil. Think as little of it as you can, my darling; and perhaps in time the community will see its own folly, and return to the true life."

"Well, I am almost glad that it is coming win-ter, that I may make the weather and my health an excuse for not going out. I can not forget my Puritan education, Richard, far enough to as-sociate with those women without a shudder of dislike."

"You must remember that they are deceived, that they do wrong just when trying most earnestly to do right. Many of them are forced into their present circumstances, and are unhappy enough to merit your pity."

"And I do pity them," said the happy, beloved wife.

After this, Margaret made bad weather and delicate health an excuse for staying closely at home. She treated all who came to see her with that kindness which was a part of her nature, but she had no real association except with two or three cultivated families, where but one wife presided over the household, and who had tastes and habits similar to her own. Her time was nearly all occupied, as she kept no help, except a little girl of thirteen, who did the coarsest of the work, and her basket was always full of sewing, ready for her leisure moments. Some little garments which laid therein may have been indebted to her home-sickness for many an elaborate pattern patiently wrought out.

"All the pride of the flesh, and wicked in the sight of God, the putting so much work on a baby's clothes;" so one of her pious and meddling neighbors informed her.

But Margaret loved to look at the little wardrobe, made beautiful by countless stitches of her embroidery-needle. It gladdened her heart, and solaced many a lonely hour when Richard was away. He was scarcely at home at all, except evenings, his business was becoming so engrossing; and she would have grown home-sick beyond endurance had it not been for this labor of love. The knowledge that he had invested his money profitably, and was getting rich; that when the city grew, as its enthusiastic inhabitants believed it would, to be the grandest city in the world—the gathering-together place of the saints all over the earth, the dazzling focus of all the rays of true glory upon earth, the future home of the immortals—he would be one of the foremost of regal and magnificent princes of the Lord's people, was the ever-present consolation for the time and thought he was obliged to give in order to work out his purpose. Much as she loved him, she could not hear these things from his lips without a secret trembling of mistrust and apprehension in that heart which possessed a woman's intuition.

When Christmas came, it found Margaret the

mother of a healthy and beautiful boy. When Richard came home, as he did three or four times a day as long as she was confined to her bed, and looked at the fair young wife fast gaining her strength and bloom again, and the little child lying sweetly upon her bosom, and realized that they were both his—his priceless treasures—he deemed himself a proud and contented man.

"I thought you as lovely as you could be when you were a timid girl and I scarcely dare kiss your reluctant hand," he said, in those accents of praise so dear to a young mother; "but you are far more beautiful now; you are *my* Margaret now, and this is our child, for which I bless you."

The happy and important news, with tidings of the welfare of all, were written home, and dispatched by the first messengers who wended their weary way back to civilization.

Margaret was seldom home-sick now. This new charge absorbed her interest and love. It was only when she thought, "What would father say to such a great fair boy as this? Oh, if mother could see the darling would n't she go wild with joy?" and, "Ah, if they could see how fast he grows,"

9

and "what darling little curls" and "deep blue
eyes," etc., etc.—after the fashion of mothers with
their first babies—that she pined very much for
her old home.

The baby was, in truth, a fine child.   The most
spiteful mother of squint-eyed, cross, or scraggy
children, would have been compelled to admit
that Mrs. Wilde's boy, Harry—as they called him
after brother Harry—was a beauty.

Surely those little delicate robes were none too
pretty for *such* a baby ; so that even the pious
neighbor who had twitted her of the "pride of
the flesh," acknowledged that he looked "dredlful
handsome" in them.

CHAPTER VIII.

THE most unhappy of all the friends who witnessed the departure of Margaret and Richard from their native village, on that twentieth day of March, was Harry Fletcher. His eyes had kept guard over Sarah all the morning, and when she fainted in his sister's arms he did not wait to see her recover, but mounted his horse and rode back at full speed to the farm. There he dashed into the hardest work he could find, and labored furiously all day long. Margaret and he had always been so tenderly attached that no one thought strange of his gloom.

As soon as it was dark, he started for Mr. Irving's. When he knocked at the door, the servant-girl came to him, and told him that Miss Irving was not well enough to see any one that evening.

"I saw her walking in the portico about five minutes ago, so I know she is up," was the reply. " Tell her I must see her a few moments, this evening—I will not detain her long."

As it was bright moonlight, Sarah came out on the porch where he was, a shawl wrapped about her to keep off the chilly March wind. She found her lover walking slowly back and forth; he did not pause or speak when she first appeared, but after two or three moments he stopped, and they stood facing each other.

"I can not endure this any longer, Sarah; this night must put an end to it. You have not made me a contented man with our engagement."

He tried to speak calmly, but the quiver in his voice told how deeply he was agitated. For a moment she looked conscience-stricken; but her untamed spirit was not the one to brook words of anger and reproach, and she curled her full lip slightly as she replied—

"I know not of what you complain. If you are

not happy, and wish to break the engagement, it is not for me to object."

"I complain of your capricious conduct toward me."

"I did not promise that I would never be too gay or too gloomy ; I did not promise to subdue all my moods to the wish of a tyrannical lover— nor will I."

"Well! I do not ask you to. I come to say that, being now thoroughly convinced of the un- happy reason for your dissatisfied heart, I come to resign all claims upon that which was never mine."

The look of disdain passed away as the young girl stood, with changing color, silently beneath his eye.

"I wish, also, to remind you that I never asked your love but once; that you then refused it, but afterward, of your own free will, you offered it to me."

"And oh, I *tried* to keep my pledge," said the girl.

"I do not blame you for your unfortunate at- tachment. It was formed, I doubt not, before you had reason to regard it as hopeless. I only pity you—and myself."

"I assure you that it was encouraged—yes, Harry Fletcher, miserably as my pride dislikes to acknowledge it, I was deceived into the belief that the love which finally settled upon another was about to become mine. I had a hard struggle to conceal my disappointment. I thought myself more proud, more strong. I have been wretchedly weak—I despise myself, at times. I have wished always that I could love you, for my own sake, as well as yours. It was with an earnest, prayerful wish and belief that I should yet regard you, as you deserve, a pure desire to make you happy, and to conquer my own waywardness, that I offered myself to you. I was determined that you should never see any want of devotion on my part, and I trusted that soon I should be all yours in truth as I was in appearance. I have not succeeded as I ought; I have wronged you, I know; but, ah! you can not have been any more troubled about it than I have been."

"I do not blame you, Sarah; I love you too well to blame you," he said, in a softened tone. "I grieve for you as much as for myself. But every sentiment of manly pride or honor within me re-

volts at the idea of binding myself to one who mar-
ries me out of compassion, and who not only does
not love me, but does love another."

"I do not love him any longer," burst forth
Sarah, eagerly. "The last chain snapped to-day.
I have been upon my knees almost all day in my
chamber, praying to God for forgiveness of my past
weakness. I have humbled my proud heart before
Him; and now I must beg that you, too, will forgive me all the wrong I have done your feelings—
all the waywardness I have shown. Say that you
will."

"Your words leave me nothing to forgive."

"I dare not ask you to show any further mercy;
and yet I do not know that I shall be able to
sustain myself alone. I feel that if you withdraw your love and esteem from me at this time,
and give me no hope of ever being able to retrieve
the past, that I shall perhaps sink back into my old
wretchedness. Bear with me a little longer, and
love will take the place of gratitude. It will be my
first real love, too," she added; "the other was a
kind of bewilderment at accomplishments and
graces which captivated my youthful fancy—a mad

passion—not the earnest and steadfast affection
which is founded upon esteem."

She stood in the moonlight with downcast eyes.

He hesitated; but beauty worked the same Cir-
ceian spell which it has wrought a million times
before. He looked upon the brightness which he
had made up his mind to resign, and his judgment
was no longer free to make its decisions. He felt
that it was more than probable that those passionate
and changeful impulses would yet bring him unhappiness; but he would dare all for the glorious prize.

"I hardly dream that I am wise, or that we shall
be happy, Sarah. Without you I surely would be
miserable. If Lucifer stood between us, I would
run the risk. You are all that I think of or hope
for; then why should I deny myself your presence?
I came here to-night resolved that I should leave
you forever—your words have not left me the
power to do so. You must be mine; you must
never shrink away from me again. Oh, Sarah! you
would be awe-stricken if you knew how I loved
you. I can never endure any more mockery or
suspense. But you will never mock me again?
never torture me with any more averted eyes, or

repelling words? You will always be as gentle, as good, as you are this moment?"

He held her hand so tightly, he gazed into her face so hopefully, and with such breathless eagerness, that she trembled beneath his eyes.

"Let us go in and sit by the fire," she said. "I feel better able to see company than I did when you knocked at the door," she added, with one of her most brilliant smiles.

They went in, and spent a long evening together. Harry did but little of the talking. His companion exerted herself as she had never done before to be kind and attractive. She assumed an irresistible gayety, just touched with a pensive shade still lingering from their first conversation. Harry abandoned himself to the pleasure she inspired; and when he left her that night, the day was appointed for the wedding.

When Sarah went to her room that night she bent herself in earnest prayer for a long time. She asked for strength to complete the good work which she had begun; to banish from her mind every lingering memory of a passion now as sinful as it was hopeless; and to cultivate in its place the af fection so richly merited by the one to whom she was so soon to be wedded; and that night she slept the untroubled slumber of peace and innocence.

Had she continued this struggle with the faults and perversities of her nature, they might have been converted into beauties. Warm-hearted, generous, charitable, extremely kind to the poor and the sick, self-forgetful, her many good qualities excited the admiration of her friends, and made them pass over her hasty temper, her pride, and her strange ways of doing strange things, which nobody else would dare to do. Her high spirits and quick wit made her follies seem lovable. No one had ever restrained her; and, alas! poor child! when, for the first time, she set seriously to work to restrain and govern herself, she found it a sad task. Many times she was discouraged with herself; many times she shed repentant tears, in the secrecy of her chamber, over the capriciousness which led her to torment her lover.

One concession she made to the wrong; from one dim chamber of her soul she shut away the light of conscience, until she could not see that there was error and danger in the dreams and fancies which lingered there. This fatal concession, this fatal error, was, that while she kept strict guard over her *actions*, she allowed her reveries, her day-dreams, to dwell in weird, revolted realms which refused allegiance to the holy land of law and order—the magic spheres of *what might have been* and *what still was possible.* And these it was that, by subtle and slow enchantments, wiled her unconsciously, step by step, from firm land into unreal realms of misty falsehood; a mist arose and clouded her moral perceptions; but it was tinged with purple and gold from the glow of passion, and she saw that it was beautiful, and would not see that it was unreliable.

About this time—most sadly, most unfortunately —there came into her hands some of the books and papers which are now being sown broad-cast over our land, and which, wherever their doctrines have taken root, have cursed the ground with thistles and thorns, instead of blessing it with the lilies and roses of purity and love. She read about "Free-Love" and "Psychological Twinships," "Passional Attractions," etc., etc.—all made enticing by fair and proper language, and not seldom invested with the glory and fascination of genius.

The works of two or three women of genius, who have polluted the gifts which God graciously bestowed upon them, and repaid Him for the treasures He intrusted to them, by giving out base, adulterated coin for pure gold—who have expressed only poison from the bright flowers of their fancy, and pressed it, with smiles of eloquence, to youthful lips —were eagerly perused and re-perused by hei, until her heart was filled with feverish unrest. May the souls of all the fair and innocent, who, like Sarah Irving, have had their youthful imaginations and youthful passions corrupted by *such* influence, rise up in all their terrible sorrow in the clear future, and accuse these women of all their loss and misery!

A work more adverse to the true mission of woman they could not have set themselves to do. It is as if angels, who have pure vessels of incense, breathing fragrance and delight upon all who approached, should fill them up with the fires and flames of the lower world, and tempt other spirits to taste, unawares, of the draughts which would blight them eternally.

If it were only men who did this wretched work,

it would be sad enough; but when women turn tempters! it fills one with a shuddering horror, as when the witch Genevieve took the innocent Christabel into her arms and against her bosom.

The wedding-day was not to be until the second week in September, so that Sarah had the whole summer before her for preparation. While sitting sewing in her chamber, she had too many lonely hours for dangerous dreams. She grew thin, and the color in her cheek too fluctuating for perfect health.

Harry had no reason to complain of her conduct toward him. She grew more and more gentle and kind, yielding to his lightest wishes, and exerting herself to please him. Yet there was an apathy in her expression when in repose, a failing of spirits and strength, which dissatisfied him.

"You do not look as well, nor as gay, as you used to, Sarah," he would say, anxiously.

"Am I not always a little thinner in warm weather? and had I not ought to begin to assume dignity and gravity, with my new position staring me so closely in the face?"

9

Her smiles, her jests, and her woman's tact, deceived him. He allowed himself to love her with all the depth and fullness of his being, and to anticipate his swift-coming joy with all the ardor of unclouded hope.

Both families were pleased with the contemplated union. Mrs. Fletcher longed for the day when Margaret's bosom-friend—" her sister," as she often used to call her—would come to them as Harry's wife, and revive something of the old gayety in the homestead.

A wing-room was built on to the mansion, with a little portico before it, commanding a pleasant view, and furnished very prettily, expressly for the young couple.

Sarah went away to Boston once or twice to purchase her trousseau, for she was fond of elegant apparel, and had a full purse of her own. It was a great treat to any of her girl companions to be admitted into her chamber and feast their eyes upon the rich and beautiful articles which filled the drawers and closets.

By interesting herself in all the splendor of preparation, and looking forward with pleasure to the effect her own beauty and fashion would have upon all, the attention she would receive as a bride, and the important part she should play in the ceremonies, she half-beguiled herself to think that love, instead of vanity, was the ruling passion.

Her uncle, being well pleased with her choice, wished to give her a splendid wedding. He had a large house, and he wanted it full of guests. As the day drew nigh, the kitchen was filled with new help, while dress-makers abounded in the sitting-room and chambers; new curtains were hung, and lamps and vases added to the store; all that there was choice in the country was engaged for the feast, and the neighbors made ready to enjoy it.

At last the wedding-day arrived; and as it drew to a close, guests from far and near gathered into the mansion, from whose every window bright lights streamed out upon the lawn and through the shrubbery. Servants hurried hither and thither, and occasionally a burst of music came upon the air preparatory to the merry strains which were to sound after the marriage supper.

The bride was in her room. She had, with her usual peculiarity of proceeding, refused to have any bridesmaids, and insisted upon making her toilet unassisted.

Half an hour before the time appointed for the ceremony, her aunt knocked at her door, and asked if she wished any aid, and receiving no reply, went away, returning in fifteen minutes to say that Harry was waiting to speak with her, and that the minister was in the house.

Upon entering the chamber, she was astonished to find that Sarah was not there, and that her toilet was not yet made. The white silk dress, with its lace trimmings, the beautiful wreath and vail, the handkerchief, the slippers, and all the little adornments, were spread out in rich array, ready to adorn the bride; but she herself was not there.

"She will be late, as she always is," exclaimed the good lady, fairly vexed. "Every one here and waiting, and she not begun to dress yet! Such a will-o'-the-wisp. What can have become of her?"

She bustled from room to room in search of the tardy bride. She was not up stairs. She went down into the dining-room and kitchen: she was not there; out into the shrubbery, and called softly "Sarah! Sarah!" but found her not, and had to go back to Harry who was waiting impatiently in his dressing-room, and tell him that she was not to be seen or heard of.

"She has not even begun to dress," she said, half angrily.

Harry turned deadly pale, and sank upon a chair.

"Good Lord! you don't think any thing could have happened to her?" exclaimed Mrs. Irving, frightened by his look.

"I do not know, I do not know. Perhaps she is in her room by this time. Let us go and see."

The whole terrible truth had struck upon the young man's mind at once, yet he could give no particular reason for it, and he would not believe it. He staggered up stairs after the lady, blind with the sudden rush of the blood from his heart, not daring to think what he feared, and yet knowing his fate, by intuition, all the time.

She was not there!

Distracted by Harry's dreadful look, Mrs. Irving did not wait as long as she should otherwise have done, but gave the alarm at once, and immediately every body was in confusion, hurrying to and fro, running with lights about the garden and the lawn,

10

rushing over to the nearest houses, looking at each other in troubled wonder, guessing, wondering, fearing.

As time sped on and the missing girl did not appear, some went to the village in search, some here and some there; some sat down and waited, and the aunt wept and wrung her hands, and the uncle tried to comfort her.

As for Harry Fletcher, he sat in the bride's apartment and made no attempt to aid in the search. No one dared to offer him a word of con-jecture or consolation. He took no notice of any thing, but sat staring at the bed where that beau-tiful dress of snowy silk, those slippers and gloves, and that bridal vail lay.

The long, long, wretched hours of that night dragged themselves away; the guests gradually dispersed; the feast remained untouched; the mu-sicians departed; and only two or three faintly glimmering lights, and two or three broken hearts, remained of all that grand display to welcome in the gray and miserable dawn.

The next morning all was learned of the fugitive that was known for some time after. Her money had been withdrawn from the bank where it was placed ; and a lady of youthful figure, closely vailed, had left in the eastern train of cars that evening.

It was in this secret flight that Sarah Irving proved herself a coward. Since she had persuaded herself that the step she took was right, and necessary to her happiness, she should have had the courage to avow it to her friends, met their objections, and saved them the bitter mortification which she heaped upon their heads. Their humiliation and grief would have been great enough, if she had prepared them for it ; they would have been spared a few of the keen arrows of public gossip ; it would have been an ill-enough return for all their love and too indulgent kindness if she had shown them as much confidence as would have prepared them for their loss.

But she dreaded the look of grief in her aunt's eye, and the keen questioning of an offended uncle, and most the agony she could not brook to witness, which she had prepared for a loving heart. She could bear to inflict it, but not to view the ruin of happiness which she had wrought. Yes ! she was worse than a woman-coward: she showed the weakness of guilt. And yet in her justification it might be said that her mind was not fully made up until the afternoon of the wedding-day. Until then it wavered, persuading itself this moment of the truth of its new doctrines, and the next, shrinking from the distress her acting upon it must cause. Bitterly she blamed herself for her changeful conduct toward Harry Fletcher—that she had not had the resolution to reject his addresses at once and forever. That she had been moved by kind impulses mattered nothing in the end, now that she must finally retract all: they only made her final resolve more blamable.

As the sun began to tinge the east with crimson and gold, Harry left the room where he had sat the night out, and without a word to any one, went home. His mother followed him; she had waited for him all night. He came to breakfast when it was ready, that none should say he was either love-sick or heart-broken. A sad and dreary change had come over his sunny and beaming face; a sternness and pride that defied pity; it almost killed his mother to see it there upon that honest, handsome brow, and if she had not been restrained by the precepts of Christ's religion, she would almost have cursed the fickle beauty who had worked the transformation.

"Father," said he, before the breakfast was finished, "I want five hundred dollars, if you can spare it; I am going to California. Nay, mother, it is useless to talk. This is no place for me. I will come back and see you, some time, but I am going from here, now."

And in less than a week he had gone. The room which was built and furnished for the expected bride was locked up, and no one entered there.

CHAPTER IX.

" What thronging, dashing, raging, rustling;
What whispering, babbling, hissing, bustling;
What glimmering, spurting, stinking, burning,
As heaven and earth were overturning.
There is a true witch element about us!
Take hold on me or we shall be divided—
Where are you ?"

GOETHE'S " FAUST."

A BAND of Mormon women were sitting in council upon the character of Margaret Wilde.

" She's quite too high and mighty for us poor sinners—she holds herself quite above *us*," said one little woman, scornfully.

"Her pride ought to be brought low," sententiously remarked a large, haughty-looking, harsh-featured female across the room.

"*I* don't think she is proud. I think her very gentle and amiable, and so beautiful," murmured a low voice, coming from the lips of a pale, sad, timid creature near by.

The last quality, of being beautiful, it was unwise in her generous champion to mention.

"Ay! beautiful!" cried the little woman, more scornfully than ever; "and that's what she sets herself up upon—thinks herself so fine that her husband must not look at another woman."

"It's a burning shame," sighed a young lady with black eyes.

"When I told her that I was going to be sealed to Elder Pritchard, she asked me how many wives he had, and when I told her eleven, she said it was wicked for me to throw myself away in that manner. As if I was not the best judge of that!" continued another. "I told her then she had better not come into a society of her own free will and then take it upon herself to dictate to them."

"*I* don't believe she is a Mormon," said the large woman.

"Of course she is n't," said Elder Pritchard's twelfth wife; "she told me as much. She said she only came out of love to her husband."

"And now she wants to keep him all to herself, and flout him in our faces, as if we were not as good as she!" exclaimed the little woman, jerking back her head.

"Why should n't she?" faintly inquired the melancholy one.

"And he is so handsome! She ought to have a lesson read to her," continued black eyes.

'I move that a committee wait upon her and suggest the propriety of her selecting a woman to be sealed to him," said the large woman. "The wives sometimes make the choice, when they are amiable enough."

"Good!" cried the little woman; "I'm dying to hear what she will say. How it will cut her up! Let us go this very afternoon. Who will be spokesman?"

"I will!" said the great woman.

"O, don't!" pleaded the sad one; but nobody heard her.

About half an hour after this, as Maggie sat, with her five-month's-old baby on her lap, in a perfect glee of merry laughter to hear him crow and laugh, and see him show some new signs of infantile intelligence, there came a knock at the door. With cheeks flushed and smiling, curls in disarray, and looking like a very lovely and very happy mother, she opened the door to usher in a formidable array of six of her most disagreeable acquaintances. However, she gave them seats, and commenced making some pleasant remarks, when she was interrupted by the speaker of the committee.

"We have waited upon you, Mrs. Wilde," she began, "to suggest the propriety of you, as the wife of an influential man among us, to set a good example, by choosing from among your acquaintance some young woman that you may fancy, to seal to your husband. It will be a means of quieting remark, and will prove you to be really interested in our religion. We think you will find our advice good," and she glanced at the black eyes which were cast down in some confusion.

For a moment the hot blood glowed richly in the cheek of Margaret; her eyes flashed proudly upon the presumptuous group, but she immediately detected, from the expression of their malicious faces, that their object was to provoke her; and so, of course, she would not be provoked.

"Well, ladies," she replied, very mildly and affably; "if Mr. Wilde wishes another wife, I would a little rather he should make the choice

himself. I have been out so little that I should
not be as well prepared to choose as he must be.
I shall be quite willing to submit to his wishes—
and to his taste;" and she, too, smiled upon the
black eyes which were regarding her curiously.

There did not seem any thing more to be said,
as her statement was very reasonable. They knew
very well that the reason she was willing was
because she was certain that her husband could
not be persuaded to make a choice. They had not
succeeded in either distressing her, or mortifying
her, or making her look miserable, at which they
felt very badly indeed, and could console themselves but very slightly by making several ill-
natured remarks about what would be expected
of members who did their duty, etc., etc. Mrs.
Wilde kept her temper undisturbed, and dismissed
them with concealed triumph, conscious that not a
barb they had sent had hit her at all. It was slyly
observed by the rest, who were in the mood for
being observing, that the young lady with the
black eyes was particularly sharp and satirical after
they had come away.

Margaret had come off from this attack with so

much self-possession, and so completely the winner
of the day, that she could afford to laugh gleefully
when she told Richard about the committee, while
they were enjoying their quiet tea.

"Human nature—human nature," he said, laughing with her; "poor human nature; it is the same
the world over, only differently developed. Jealous, inquisitive, discontented women, ready to tear
you to pieces because you are good and beautiful."

"How can they be otherwise than jealous and inquisitive, situated as they are, poor creatures? I
do not think I ought even to be resentful."

"Whatever has helped to make them so, I am
afraid they will give us some inconvenience in the
course of time. Just as I was about to step into
some lucrative office, I should hate to have
one of these elders' wives making a fuss about
me."

"Why will you stay where there is such an
abominable state of society, dear Richard?" Margaret asked, suddenly growing very earnest. "Oh,
you do not know how unhappy it makes me at
times, to be mixed up with it. I would rather lose
all that we have made, and go back to our old

home without a penny, than to think of spending my life here."

"Pooh! pooh! my darling! are we not society enough for ourselves, and with the baby there? Why can you not give yourself no thought about it? and in a few years we will be living in such a way that the crowd can not get very close to you. We will have a palace in the suburbs, and such a lawn and such a grove about it, that the world will be shut out. You shall have fountains, and birds, and exquisite flowers about you; and your beautiful boy and your adoring husband for company.

> "'In Zanadu did Khubla Khan
> A stately pleasure-dome decree.'
> "In Utah did the saintly Richard
> A stately pleasure-dome decree,
> Wherein his fair wife placéd he."

But the tears were in Margaret's eyes while he spake.

"I am sorry that you can not overlook the one fault of this people, Margaret," added Richard, more earnestly. "They are truly a wonderful people; they have made 'the wilderness blossom as the rose;' they have conquered all obstacles; and their religion is so fascinating, so inspiriting. We have 'signs and wonders,' Margaret—the Spirit of the Lord poured out upon us as free as water. We are indeed His favored children : this city shall be greater than Jerusalem ever was. Our streets shall some time be paved with gold, and our walls shall glitter with precious stones. A palace shall arise for you and I, as by the spell of Aladdin's lamp. Our tabernacle shall be a miracle of glory. It may not all take place in our life-time, rapid as is the gathering in of the Latter-Day Saints. But we shall arise from the grave to welcome it, and live a thousand years of love and joy in the City of the Lord. Oh! what a thing our love is, Margaret, when we remember that we are to enjoy it together a thousand years! Let not trifles distract you from that glorious anticipation. Here we are safe; our salvation is secured; and would you have me an unsettled wanderer about the world? Are you not glad that we are safe in the fold?"

Margaret sobbed aloud with conflicting emotions: pain that her husband could be deluded by the rant and false show of a religion which grew more distasteful to her all the time; and hope, that even this

10

wretched belief was better, if it was sincere, than blank doubt and infidelity.

"Now, Maggie, are n't you growing a little nervous? I am afraid the care of that great boy is too much for you. To-night, at all events, you must leave him to Susan, and the dishes to her, also, and go to the temple with me. It's a long time since you were out, and the sisters are jealous of you. Besides, I am to be appointed an elder this evening. I shall be Elder Wilde after this, dear; how will it sound? and you must not be absent. It is but the first stepping-stone, and I value it as such. Some time I shall be where Brigham Young is now," he added, rising from the table, and pacing back and forth across the floor in an excited manner; "and it may be that some time this people will see fit to have a temporal ruler—a king! throned in all the magnificence of Solomon. That is what *I* shall try for."

"Oh, Richard!" exclaimed his wife, in fear and reproach.

"Not unless the Lord wills it," he continued, hurriedly, fearful lest he had betrayed too much to the quick eye of affection. "But if a thing is appointed, why not I be anxious to serve the Lord?"

Ah, Religion! what ambition, what pride, what covetousness, what cruelty, what hate, what wickedness, hath not sheltered itself under thy cloak!

Mrs. Wilde arose with a sigh to prepare to go with her husband. He caught her hand as she passed out of the room, and looked admiringly into her face.

"I know that I have the tact and the ability to rule such a community for their own good," said he; "and as for you, Margaret, Esther could not have been a more beautiful queen than you will make."

"Oh, my husband, put such thoughts far away from you," she replied; "the love of power is not the love of God."

"But if God should choose me out as an instrument in His hands to work His glory?"

Margaret turned away with a trembling lip; and after giving directions to Susan, the small girl she had to help her, to be sure and stay by the baby, she put on her bonnet, and accompanied her husband to the temple. She felt a weight upon her spirits as she walked along, which was somewhat dissipated, as they entered the great building, by its gorgeous appearance, illuminated with lights. Margaret took a seat amid a good many others, while Richard went forward to be initiated into his duties as elder. After that was over, some one of the presidents preached a sermon upon the future prospects of the Mormons, also reproving some of the bishops and elders for selfishness and non-payment of tithes, and finally got upon the subject of miracles. Said he:

"We were speaking about an open vision which we saw some time ago—it was seen in the dark, but we saw it with our natural eyes. President Young, myself, brother Phineas Young, and many others, saw it. We saw an army start from the east and go to the south, and there were twelve men in a column, and one column came right after the other, so that when the first stepped, the next stepped in their tracks, and so on; and they had swords, guns, knapsacks, caps and feathers, and we could see them march, with a uniform step, from one heavens to the other. This we saw with our natural eyes, and looked upon it for hours—it was the very night that the angel delivered the plates to Joseph Smith. This army moved to the south-west, and they marched as if a battle were to take place; and we could hear the clashing of their swords and guns, and the measured tread of their march, just as plain as I ever heard the movements of troops upon the earth. John P. Green came to wake me up to look upon it."

From this he drew an augury of war, in which the Mormons were to be triumphant; then he had a few warning words to say to those who were not believers, asking them to hold up their hands and declare themselves; then, no hands being raised, he promised the faithful a miracle—upon the heads of the most exalted saints should glow a crown of light, in token of their future high estate, when they should be crowned everlastingly. Hereupon there was a high state of excitement and expectation amid the congregation. The first step toward the accomplishment of the miracle was the putting out of all the lights in the temple; a solemn silence reigned for a few moments, and, one by one, circles of lambent light began to play around the heads of the throng. Suppressed whispers of praise

11

and glorification, with murmurs of prayer, resound-
ed through the vast tabernacle. Soon the lamps
were re-lit, and the awed and astonished people began to breathe more freely.

Elder Pratt had then a few words to say on polygamy:

"I hereby pledge my honor that I will publicly
renounce polygamy, and that the Church I repre-
sent will do the same, on the following conditions,
namely: The Old and New Testaments, the Constitution of the United States, and the laws of Utah
Territory, shall be the standard; and if, in all this
wide range, one item of law can be found wherein
God, angels, men, apostles, prophets, or the Son of
God, or the Holy Spirit, have made the plurality of
wives a crime, or transgression of law, or an immo-
rality, then, on these conditions, we shall renounce
polygamy. But, till this is done, we shall hold the
law of God on the subject of matrimony, including
a plurality of wives, as a most sacred institution,
binding on our consciences, in the free exercise of
which we claim the protection so freely guarantied
by the constitution of our common country."

After some music the congregation were dismissed. Richard joined his wife in fine spirits; but all that she 'had heard and seen had only excited her suspicion and disgust, and she walked by his side in thoughtful silence.

"Come, dear, why don't you talk? What is the matter? Are you not glad that I am an elder?"

"I should be if I believed in this religion, Richard; but it looks like a farce and a mockery to me. I am certain that they used phosphorus or some chemical preparation to get up that miracle to-night. Tell me what is your true opinion?"

"What a question!" was the evasive reply.

"It was a shameful imposture upon credulous ignorance," continued Margaret, more warmly.

"You must not breathe such a sentiment as that aloud," said Richard, somewhat alarmed. "Come, wife, I am afraid you are getting a little unreasonable. You must remember what will be expected of one in my place."

She did not wish to displease him, and she said no more; but a foreboding came across her, that perhaps, some time, his ambition would be his mistress—that he would love power more than his wife.

Oh, how fondly she took her baby to her bosom when she got into the house, yearning over it with an undefined sadness.   But when Richard came, and encircled her and the infant in one tender embrace, kissing first one, and then the other, and calling them "pet names," she forgot her presentiments.

CHAPTER X.

"Daughter of Egypt! veil thine eyes,
    I can not bear their fire,
    Nor will I touch with sacrifice
        Those altars of desire."

                        BAYARD TAYLOR.

IT was a warm day in the latter part of June—warm, and yet delightful, for a cool breeze swept the plains, and passed like a blessing over the city.

The wild-rose, which Margaret had trained by her door and window, tossed its blossoms about, and their faint fragrance filled the apartment with delight. She sat near the casement reading the papers which had arrived by the mail which came in that morning; a letter she had already perused a dozen times—a letter from Harry, written in the name of his father and mother, as well as himself—and speaking in glowing terms of his anticipated happiness. It was nearly a year old, having lain at Council Bluff through the winter.

"I suppose Harry and Sarah are married long

ago. How I wish I could peep in upon them one day—just one day—and show them our baby, Richard," she had said at the dinner-table, while they were discussing the letter and all the old familiar topics which it brought up.

Now, while she had a leisure hour or two, she was enjoying the paper and a magazine—a rare treat, indeed, to her. Her child was sleeping sweetly in the neat bedroom, whose door stood open that the mother might have an eye upon the slumbers of her darling.

Susan came in and laid the cloth for tea, and soon Richard appeared. As the biscuits were not quite done, the wife read aloud to him until they were ready.

"There was a large band of new Saints arrived to-day with the mail-train," remarked Richard, as they sat up to the table.

"Were any of them from our part of the country?" was the first eager inquiry.

"I think not. They came from Western New York, I believe, the most of them, with a few English.

"Oh, dear! I had almost hoped to see some one

who had seen or heard of our friends," sighed Margaret.

A moment after a shadow darkened the sunlight which lay across the threshold; and the shadow reached forward and rested upon Margaret's bosom, where a little gleam of golden light had been dancing. The young couple looked up—they looked twice before they spoke—and then sprung to their feet.

"It is!" exclaimed Richard.

"Yes, it is Sarah Irving!" cried his wife—and for a moment they could say no more.

There she stood, looking at them with a half smile, though her own heart beat to suffocation. Her cheeks were suffused with blushes, and she, too, was as speechless as they. Richard was the first to reach her; he took her in his arms and gave her a kiss; it was so long since he had seen an old friend, that he embraced her as he would have done his mother.

"You are very tired," he said, as he observed how heavily she lifted herself from his breast.

"Yes," she whispered; and then she and her old school-friend, Margaret, met in a long embrace.

"But where is Harry?" asked the latter, suddenly raising her head from Sarah's shoulder.

"He is not here; I came alone."

Surprise and curiosity began to take the place of
joy and astonishment; but they would ask no questions until they had taken off the bonnet and cape of
their guest, seated her at the table and placed a cup
of barley coffee before her, for she seemed tired and
agitated.

She drank the coffee and seemed to feel more
composed. Her friends gazed at her as if they
could not realize that they were indeed beholding
the face of their beloved Sarah

"I was a sunburnt and deplorable-looking creature when I arrived here, darling; but I do believe
that nothing can ever injure or intimidate you; you
look better than ever," said Margaret, gazing with
her old fondness into the countenance of her visitor.

The sun and winds had given her clear complex-
ion a richer glow; they had given her cheeks the
same bright flush which they give the crimson rose;
her eyes had a lustrous depth, dark and unfathoma-
ble; her hair was as wild as the wild vine, and as
beautiful; and her gipseyish dress added a charm

to her appearance quite in keeping with her style.

"O, I enjoyed the whole journey very much, hardships and all," she added gayly. "Every thing except seeing three men killed, and two women carried off by a band of Sioux, who came upon us suddenly. Oh, but I wanted a gun in my hands then! I had this knife in my bosom," she added, drawing out a small bowie-knife from her dress, "fearing I might have occasion to defend myself, but, thank heaven, I was not obliged to use it."

"Do tell me, Sarah, what brought you here without Henry; I can not wait another instant to know about my brother."

She cast down her eyes as she answered—

"I became a Mormom, and he did not."

"And oh, did you have the heart to come away and leave him? He loved you so, Sarah, so deeply, I know. I thought you were married long ago."

"We were to have been married, but I should have been wicked—have rendered him as well as myself miserable if I had kept my too-illy considered promise. I *could not* love him as a wife ought to, and you know, you only, dear Maggie, that I *tried* to return his affection, but, why did he love me?" she cried in a trembling voice, "I was never worthy of so good a man."

"Ay, why did he?" echoed Mrs. Wilde, very bitterly for her.

"But we must go where our hearts call us," continued the other, fixing her dark eyes, burning through their tears, upon Richard, as she spoke in a low, impassioned tone, "and mine has called me here with a wild, earnest call which I can not choose but obey."

"And you, too," murmured Margaret, "the victim of this strange, this foolish fanaticism!"

"I was born for an enthusiast—I only love what is strange, and new, and incomprehensible; or what is too high, or too far away for us to achieve," and again her eyes sought Richard's.

He remembered the last look those eyes had given him, as they parted long ago, and she turned to faint upon Margaret's bosom—that thrilling, agonized look—and somehow he could not but connect it with the glances she gave him now, and the blood rushed into his cheek at a thought which came unbidden.

"Oh, Sarah, Sarah!" said Margaret mournfully, "I have so much to forgive in you, it is a wonder that I can love you at all. My poor brother!"

"I *am* unworthy of your affection, Maggie; I had no right to come here to your house; I have no claim upon your kindness. I only came to give you news of home, and then I shall trouble you no more."

She reached for her bonnet as she said this; grieved and wounded though she was, distressed at the thought of Henry, his sister could not find it in her heart to utterly cast out her friendship for Sara; she knew her impulsiveness, her want of proper training; she blamed, but she loved at the same time; so she carried the bonnet into the bedroom, and coming back, kissed the perverse girl, and asked to be told all about home.

Sarah gave an account of things as they were before she left—*not*, as they must have been, after that event. She told them their parents were in good health and spirits, and that, although she could not doubt that Harry felt very badly, yet he had not *seemed* to be very much disappointed, and she had no doubt he would some time forget her, and find a companion better suited to render him happy. She did not confess the cruel manner in which she had deserted him; she dared not do it; and she hoped before the news reached them, to have gained a foothold into the Eden she desired, from which she could not be driven.

While they were all busy asking and answering eager questions, the baby awoke and began to cry.

"What's that?" asked Sarah, growing pale.

"You are not frightened at the sound of a child crying?" asked Margaret, laughing; "why! just think of it; I have been so absorbed in hearing from home that I forgot, absolutely forgot for almost an hour, to tell you that we have a baby!"

"A great fine boy, six months old," said Mr. Wilde proudly, while his wife ran to take little Harry from his crib.

"What do you think of this?" asked the young mother, coming back with her treasure, who had ceased his impatient petition to be taken up, and was looking his very prettiest, with his cheeks all rosy from sleeping so hard, and his hair all in tiny ringlets over his head. "Ay, Sarah? is not this doing pretty well for the first? ought I not to thank

my sweet wife for such a beauty?" and the wretched girl thought she had never seen him look so
good and so very handsome, as when he took the
little fellow in his arms, with kindling eye and joy-
ous, fatherly pride.

"It seems very strange to see you a mother, Maggie," she said faintly, smiling strangely upon the
child.

"Does n't it?" laughed Margaret, as she claimed
the boy to give him his supper.

His playful ways and his parents' delight were
viewed with a melancholy eye. Sarah could not
bear the great happiness of her friends. She had
wild thoughts; and then her better angel awoke out
of its deep sleep and arose and struggled fiercely
against the dark spirit which had taken possession
of her. One by one, the spirit brought forward its
weapons of defense, false doctrines, forged in the
flames of passion, and polished with fine cold sophistries: but they were base metal, and fell shivered
at its feet, before the subtle touch of truth. She
turned her face from the smiling group and went to
the wild-rose vines at the door and began weaving
a wreath.

11

"Don't make yourself any prettier than you are already," said Richard, as he saw what she was doing.

"Nay! this crown is for Margaret," she said, "the emblem of love, beauty, and simplicity. I am not fit to wear it."

"You speak of yourself very depreciatingly, dear Sarah," said Margaret. "I do not think you the greatest sinner in the world—though I do wish you could have loved my brother. But what's the use of wishing? You are a will-o'-the-wisp, a meteor, an aurora-borealis, any thing that is wild, beautiful, uncatchable, unreliable, fascinating. We shall have to let you glitter and sparkle, come and go, delude and bewitch us, without complaint—taking you for what you choose to hold yourself worth."

"Well, here's your wreath, to pay for that. You ought to know that I can not bear flattery."

"It plays about you like heat-lightning, neither blinding, warming, nor scorching you. Really you have made my wife look very pretty, Sarah."

"I think so myself, Sir Richard."

"Which shows that you are not envious."

Sarah looked as if she thought she need be envious of but few women; and so Richard Wilde thought, and wondered if she could have been as beautiful when he chose between her and his more gentle Margaret.

The conversation again reverted to home matters, and when, late in the evening, they retired to rest, Sarah Irving was glad to press her weary head to its pillow. It was the first time she had slept beneath a roof for many weeks, and yet her slumbers were not as sweet as they had often been in the open air with only a wagon-cover over her.

She had placed herself under the protection of the most respectable family she could find coming out; and the next day after her arrival at the Wilde's, she called upon them at their stopping-place to thank them for their past kindness.

She was welcomed into the bosom of the Mormon creed; and soon became an object of much attention to its followers. Her youth and beauty, as well as the rumor that she had brought several thousand dollars in gold along with her, were enough to ren der her a favorite, especially with the men. Many a gray-haired elder fixed covetous eyes upon her;

eyes bleared and foul, from which she shrank as
from a serpent.

It was not long before Brigham Young himself
had marked the glittering prize as his own; but she
held herself in reserve, and gave no one any encouragement, although she professed herself converted to polygamy.

There was not much said about this part of her
belief before Margaret, whose horror of the doctrine
was such, that she could hardly tolerate the companionship of its devotees; and who felt great uneasiness about the future fate of her beautiful friend
so deluded in her faith, although yet pure in action.

With consummate tact she won upon the interest
of Richard. He was her friend and counselor in
all things. She had a great many things to do, and
she wished him to aid her in all. First, she set
about having her a house built; it was to be the
finest dwelling-house in the city, and she wanted it
finished before winter. There were plenty of labor-
ers to be had to do the work quickly and well. She
ordered the best furniture which could be manufac-
tured there; and as there were no carpets to be had,
she set some foreigners who understood it, to weav-

ing matting out of a long, reedy grass which she found. People smiled, and praised her energetic ways of bringing what she wished to pass. A part of her money she lent to Richard for some purpose which he desired; another part she had him invest for her, and the rest she kept to pay for her house, and do with as she happened to fancy.

She bought her a pony like Margaret's, and spent half her time roaming over the country after wild-flowers and berries. No Indian maiden of the forest rode her steed with a wilder grace, or decked herself out more gorgeously with flowers and scarlet leaves; she would ride like the winds across the plains, or sit quietly on her horse and send forth her sweet, clear voice in trills of melody, such as were never heard in that remote wild before.

Week after week flitted by; the house, which was a good distance from her friends', was progressing rapidly; and one evening after tea, she wanted Richard to walk over with her, to see if any improvements could be planned. It stood away beyond the suburbs, not too far to be included within the walls of Zion, when they should be determined, and in a most lovely spot.

12

A rise of ground, with a group of trees already grown upon it, commanding a view of the city, dark mountains rising beyond in one direction, and in another the waters of the lake gleaming in the distance, was the spot selected by Sarah. About ten acres of the surrounding fair and breezy grounds constituted her domains; when the city spread she did not wish to be shut away from the trees and the green grass entirely, and so she had purchased these ten acres in which to belt her house.

They climbed up the ladder into the unfinished chambers, and sat a few moments in the window commanding the loveliest prospect.

"I mean to go to-morrow, Sarah, and purchase the land contiguous to yours, that I may hold it in readiness to build a better house on than I have now. You showed your fine taste in this selection. It is the sweetest place about the city; the view is enchanting; it is like Paradise—lovely beyond expression."

"Ay, Richard; see the sunlight streaming over the plains, turning the lake into an ocean of burnished gold, and bathing the mountains in rosy, evanescent hues. Oh! this is the place to be wildly, madly happy in. Here, free from the cold bonds, the chilling orthodoxies of the world, with a love-breathing, kindly, fascinating religion, and lavished by the indulgent hand of nature all about us, why can not our souls revel in life as it was designed to be? why can not we be free as the winds, bright as the flowers, happy as the birds?"

Richard looked upon his eloquent companion. Her eyes burned with a soft fire, and their melting glory was poured steadily into his. She leaned toward him with a smiling countenance, her cheek was red and her lip tremulous.

"We can be—we will be," he answered her; "I will have a house here close by yours. You will marry some man that you love, and then you will realize how happy my Margaret and I are—and our boy."

The smile fled from her lip and she looked out at the distant mountains with a melancholy gaze.

'Why do you look so sad? and a moment ago you were planning such delights."

There was nothing more than kindness in his tone —possibly a shade of tenderness of which he was not conscious.

"Oh, Richard Wilde," she half sobbed, turning to him again, "I fear I shall never be married. The golden chance for me is lost; the only man I ever did, or could, or shall love was lost to me long ago. We might be happy yet, if there was more freedom in the world. But he—he would be afraid, he would startle at the thought of drinking the cup of heavenly nectar pressed to his lips. Would there were less bigotry, less cold and senseless cant in the world. Oh! when will people be free to follow the divine inspiration of their own hearts? when will they cease to needlessly torture themselves? when will they learn that attractions can not err—that they may trust their own truest impulses? Even here—even here, in this fair world which is apart from the world, must this chain be worn?— Richard!"

She spoke his name in a soft, full, musical voice, most passionately sad, and laid her trembling hand lightly upon his. He looked at her in troubled surprise. He was not proof against the glowing words, the winning modulations of voice, the plead- ing eyes, the gentle touch:—a consciousness of all her meaning rushed over him, what he had often laughed at himself for suspecting, became reality; the blood rushed into his face, and to turn aside his embarassment, he asked—

"What made you a Mormon, Sarah?"

"Love!" she answered; "that is, love of novelty, of the wilds of the west, of my friends here; but most, love of something more fresh, less trammeled; I wanted to be free," and all of a sudden her manner changed, and she laughed gayly. "Pray do not pay any attention to what I say when the inspired mood is upon me. You could not understand if you would—you have not advanced far enough for that."

She tossed back her head with a motion of merry scorn. Richard thought he had never seen any thing so exquisite as her chin and throat, all dimples and lovely lines, and flushed with the rosy sunset light. Her hair waved back from her polished brow, across her delicate ears, and was caught by a ribbon and little golden comb, from thence falling upon her shoulders, in masses of glossy curls.

"You are a Sphynx," he said in return; "I do not pretend to read your riddles," for dangerously bewitching as she was, he thought of Margaret and his boy, and wanted to break the spell which was stealing over him.

"Had we not better return, Sarah? Margaret will wonder what has become of us."

"Margaret! Margaret!" she said, impatiently, "is your wife so miserly with her happiness that she can not spare you for half an hour to an old friend?"

"My wife is not lacking in generosity toward her friends," was the rather cool reply.

"Oh, no! I meant nothing against her, I love her. She is gentle, and good, and affectionate. But I doubt if she could make sacrifices for those she loves, as some can do—as some have done. She is the very model of a kind and amiable wife. If I had been like her, I might have been the contented partner of Harry Fletcher, instead of the unhappy creature that I am, wandering over freezing mountains, and burning plains, following afar off the sun that I worship, whose brightness is not for me, whose fires will never warm my chilled and desolate heart. I have thrown my life away, without the hope of reward," and again she passed into a gloomy reverie.

Richard sat gazing upon her with mingled emo-

tions. His man's vanity was not slow to point out
to him the meaning of her words. Many a look
and act in the long ago—before his marriage and
after—came back to his memory, and he was pained
and embarrassed at the truth which stared him in
the face so plainly.

Yet he was flattered too. He began to try and
image to himself the depth and worth of a passion
which gave such proofs of its consuming power. The
very pride with which the beautiful girl before him
kept others aloof and afraid of her, added to the effect upon him of her deportment toward him alone.

The request of several of his friends that he
should take another wife; and a kind of confused
impression that perhaps it *was* permitted to the
Saints to do so, recurred to him; and passion, which
blinds reason, began to act upon his judgment.
Clear and fair before his mental vision arose the image of Margaret, rocking the cradle of his child,
and the mere thought of the agony which such a
step would cause her, dispelled the mist, and left him
free to see the wrong.

So he shook the temptation lightly off.

"Come, Sarah, we really must go."

"To be sure we must; pardon me for detaining you: I was busy with my dreams."

She arose as stately as Juno; her eye was cold and bright; the feeling which had illuminated it had died out; and she went down the ladder without his assistance, and walked home by his side with a queenly step, replying briefly to his few remarks.

"Sarah has on her imperial robe and crown to-night," remarked Mrs. Wilde, shortly after the two returned.

"I rule but an empty realm," was the slow reply. "But I will have subjects enough at my feet soon. The Governor was to see me again this morning."

"I do not like to hear you even jest about him," replied Margaret. "It is so shocking that he should set the example which he does."

"I think he does just right, provided he really loves the women he chooses. If I had not been a convert to *all* the doctrines of Mormonism I should not have come here, to be made miserable by jeopardizing my happiness."

"I am not miserable, for I have entire, implicit confidence in my husband. But I am often pained, and oh, so much, to hear *you* advancing such sentiments; to feel that you are in danger of making shipwreck of your peace.   How could, *you*, with all your pride, consent to occupy an inferior, secondary situation, and have the heart of your husband divided up among a dozen others?   It would kill you. Oh, Sarah, I do implore you, by all that is most sacred, most pure, most dear, most beautiful in woman, to turn your voice and influence against this social degradation, and manifest the detestation which I am sure, in your secret soul, you must feel for it."

Sarah made her no reply, except to bid her goodnight, and retire to her own room.   She undressed, and threw herself upon the couch, but the night was oppressive, and her thoughts were more oppressive than the night.

"My resolution almost fails me," she whispered to herself.   "Margaret has been my truest friend always, and I can not be so cruel as to break her heart.   Why could she not have become a believer? then all would have gone well.   I hoped to have found her converted to this belief, and willing to receive me as I wished.   I have dared and suffered all, and now I must give up; I left two distressed and suffering households and a blighted faith behind me. I made up my mind to that much—but I had not counted upon breaking Margaret's heart."

She lay a long time with her fingers pressed over her eyes; a terrible struggle, worse than any that had ever taken place in her restless bosom, was going on between passion and conscience; she could not bring ruin upon this roof which sheltered her, she could not betray the hospitality which had welcomed her, the trusting affection of her girlhood's friend;—neither could she overcome the love which had grown from fatal nursing of it, to a mighty passion which now mocked her strength. Once, she might have held it in subjection, but she had dallied with it, put it away only to welcome it more warmly, cherished it secretly upon sweet thoughts and honeyed hopes—and now it mastered her.

It is madness to expect happiness from any but legitimate sources. Sarah Irving was suffering constantly from the punishment which followed upon every concession she made to the false philosophy she had deluded herself into accepting; yet, she would not see that her doubt and unhappiness arose from her misdoing. The dupe of her own desires, she allowed herself to be convinced that religion demanded that she should not regard what would be but the temporary grief of her friend Margaret. She could not go to heaven except as the wife of some man—she could not be the wife of any man whom she did not love—she could not love any man but Richard Wilde.

Her entrance through the gates of Paradise depended upon him, and cling to him she must. Heaven pity and comfort Margaret; she would some time see that it was right; she could not sacrifice herself to save her friend some pangs.

And so, after hours of tossing and unrest, she slept upon her resolution.

CHAPTER XI.

Ah, what shall I be at fifty,
    If nature keep me alive,
If I find the world so bitter
    When I am but twenty-five?

, TENNYSON.

THE letter written by Margaret's mother, giving an account of the strange events at home, Sarah's flight, and Harry's departure for California, never reached its destination, and the daughter knew nothing of the solitary, unhappy condition of her parents, bereft of their eldest son.

Gentle as Margaret's nature was, if she had known the whole truth about the state of affairs at home, she could hardly have tolerated the girl who had brought so much unhappiness upon the family; for she found it difficult to forgive her for breaking her engagement with her brother when she represented the matter in so much brighter light than it was.

A sad condition, indeed, had taken the place of the old prosperity at the homestead. The old couple were left pretty much alone.   Two half-grown boys, were all the children left to them.   There was but little pleasure to them in contemplating Margaret's change of circumstances.   They scarcely expected ever to see her again in this world; and they could not forget that she was with a Mormon husband in a Mormon city; and they were beginning to take note of the unenviable notoriety the Latter-day Saints were acquiring.   The letter telling them that Margaret was the mother of a lovely boy, gave them a great deal of pleasure, not unmixed with anxiety; and this was shortly followed by another, giving still more glowing accounts of their health and happiness.   But communications were often delayed or lost, and they would have weeks of suspense, always fearing the worst; for their days had darkened so, that they could not look upon things as cheerfully as of old.

Harry's bitter disappointment was almost greater than they could bear; and his sudden departure left a gloom upon the threshold which no sunshine could dispel.

The deserted bridal-chamber was the "skeleton in the house," which gave it all a haunted look.

12

There was no one to open the piano and chase away sad influences by the soft spirit of sweet sounds; no Sarah to come sparkling into the room like a bird; no Margaret to sing from morning till night, flitting about the house like a gleam of sunlight; no Harry, with his manly form, and pleasant voice, to break in upon the monotony of the hours.

The two lads were good and obedient; they made noise enough at times, too, with their boyish amusements, to frighten melancholy out of the farm-house, but they were at school the most of the day, and when at home, their society was not as agreeable as it might have been at almost any other stage of their existence.   Their mother was not a nervous woman, yet she was annoyed by their tearing into the house, fresh from some contest of skill, some game of hand-ball, or the like, which made them running over full of laughter and excitement.   She wanted silence in which to ponder over her cares.

She felt the most uneasy about Harry. He was the apple of her eye; and that he should be away in California, exposed to dangers without number, and perhaps plunging recklessly into the temptations which must beset him, was cause enough to rob her of rest.

"I do not know what we have done to bring such punishments upon us," she would say to her husband, as they sat by the fire of the long winter evenings, scarcely enjoying the apples, nuts and cider upon the little table beside them. " We have tried to bring up our children in the nurture and admonition of the Lord; we have performed our duty according to the light we have had ; and now, when old age is coming upon us, some unpleasant circumstance takes one after another away from us. There's Margaret, poor child, away by herself in the midst of that horrid people. She'll need a double share of divine grace to sustain her footsteps in the right path. And Harry ! I was so proud of him, husband—too proud of him I'm afraid now, and it may be a judgment upon me, and yet he was a child to make glad a mother's heart—how do we know what will become of him? He may take to gambling or something desperate ; for when a man's hope is gone, and his heart broken, there's not much to keep him out of wrong-doing, unless he can throw himself into the hands of the Lord.

Harry was a good man, but he had n't Christian faith enough to sustain him when he needed it the most."

And they would talk over their troubles, while the rosy-cheeked apples lay undisturbed upon the plate, and the cider bubbled and simmered upon the hearth, as if impatient to have its good qualities tested.

"Let us read the thirty-seventh Psalm," the good man would say solemnly, when nine o'clock struck, and he would read it slowly —

"Fret not thyself because of evil-doers."

Giving particular emphasis to such verses as these:

"Rest in the Lord and wait patiently for Him." "The steps of a good man are ordered by the Lord; though he fall, he shall not be utterly cast down." "I have been young, and now I am old, yet I have not seen the righteous forsaken."

In a few months they had a letter from Harry which, while it did not remove all their anxiety, was a great comfort to them.

"Do not fear, mother," he wrote, "that I shall become a bad man. I have too much self-respect to

degrade myself by evil associations or evil deeds.
I hold myself aloof from the whirl of iniquity
which sweeps away the most of the people here.
But excitement I must have—intense excitement for
a while, or I should die. Here I have it fierce and
irresistible. There is gambling going on as desperate as that in the hells which are nightly thronged
throughout the city—gambling for fortune. Her
golden wheels whirl round with inconceivable ra-
pidity, and prizes that make men dizzy come up;
and millions are won and lost each hour of the day.
Men become absorbed—fascinated. Men who are
loving and devoted to their families, forget home,
wife, children for 'the time, in this strange game;
they live an intense, concentrated life; they watch
the whirl and take their gains and losses with the
same set faces. I am one among them; it keeps me
from more maddening reflection.

"I am resolved to do nothing dishonorable, nothing for which I shall have to blush when I am myself again. Time will bring its own remedy. You
shall see me again, providence sparing my life, your
boy Harry, as he used to be; a little sterner-hearted,
less confiding, than of old—not precisely a happy
13

man perhaps, but not a misanthropist, and not a miscreant. I suffer when I think of your lonely situation; but you must spare me a little while yet. Give my love to Margaret through your letters, for I can not write to her while I feel as I do now."

CHAPTER XII.

The watch-dog howled with sudden dread:
" Oh, would my lover were here," she said.
The witch upon the wind drew near,
She bent close down to the maiden's ear.
What she said, none ever knew—
The bridesmaids thought the wind but blew.

SARAH'S house was completed; and she became
its solitary inmate, except a young girl whom she
took in to do her housework. Margaret wondered
that she should keep up an establishment of her
own, when she might just as well have had a home
with her, but yielded as usual to her whim, thinking
it must be her intention to marry, although she
could not guess who.

There were plenty who sought the hand of Miss
Irving. Some men, who had already fulfilled the
Mormon vow, of taking as many wives as they
could support, had no objections to taking another
who could support herself.

Such glory as there was in being a belle in that

community, she enjoyed to its full extent. It was all a matter of contempt and indifference to her, except that she could tell over her offers and refusals to Richard Wilde—an occupation very suggestive to him.

The autumn evenings lengthened themselves wearily out, and the still longer ones of winter came. Sarah had but few books to read, but little work to do, no music at first, although a German, who fell in love with her, made her a beautiful guitar as a Christmas gift—and time hung heavy upon her hands.

She would not go to Mrs. Wilde's much; she was far from happy there; and Margaret's rather delicate health, and the care of her boy, prevented her returning many of what visits she did make her.

With her usual disposition to give others pleasure, the young wife did not complain when her husband spent evening after evening at Sarah's house. He was exceedingly fond of playing chess, and she herself was but a poor player, while Sarah could contend with him so successfully that it was often late when he returned home.

"Poor Sarah is so lonely, and Richard loves to

play so much," she would say to herself, as she sat quite solitary in her little parlor, with only the soft breathing of her boy in his crib, to break the silence. Her own thoughts were too pure, her own love was too steadfast, ever to suggest to her that there was danger in this constant companionship of her husband and her beautiful friend.

Their Harry was a year old, and winning more of her heart every day. He could lisp a half dozen household words, and was learning to balance his dimpled feet on the floor, and to essay perilous voyages from one chair to another.

Her cup was running over with the sweetest blessings of life, and if her husband left her to spend many evenings in solitude, she used them as times of joyful reflection upon the past and future. She was so happy in her HOME! Without its walls there was but little to please, and much to annoy her; within its charmed precincts there were only peace and love and innocent joy. It seemed to her that no trouble could really perplex her, unless it intruded itself within those walls, upon the hearthstone of home.

Sickness and death were the only things the

thoughts of which sent a shadow across her brow. She was content to let the world of Mormonism without her doors, rage and storm as it would—its turbulent waves staid themselves at her door-step.

Time flitted by, bringing with every day a change in Richard Wilde. He was prospered among the people, and his ambitions grew prodigious, as he saw new ways opening before him by which, if he only discarded the strict laws which had governed him in New England, he could follow on to personal glory. He was amid those who made their own laws to suit their own purposes, who brought strange doctrines out of the depths of their own foul imaginations and called them revelations. His natural tendencies had been restrained by education and example, but now that these were torn away, his actions would not always bear the clear light of an accusing conscience; and presently, conscience no longer intruded herself.

Much fault had been found with him, that he did not fulfill his duty as a good citizen, by appropriating more women to himself, and saving their souls alive by making them his wives. But upon this one point he had remained incorruptible. He had a good angel at home who protected him. He could not so suddenly abandon the holiest and sweetest institution of Christianity and civilization, and all that there is pure and saving in the midst of the selfishness of man : one abiding love, one hearth, one home. His Margaret was all-in-all to him—his wife —the other part of himself, upon whose union with him depended the perfection of his being; the woman whom he had chosen, a modest and innocent maiden, to share his fortunes and his heart, and to be the mother of his children.

But at last, like many other men, not truthful and pure in their inmost souls, not really and earnestly in love with virtue, he was tempted by beauty where ambition alone could not have prevailed. Thoughts which had no right there began to occupy his bosom. He often contrasted Margaret's somewhat pale and thin cheek—which ought to have been a thousand times dearer to him that it had grown pale with maternal cares—with the rich, bright cheek of Sarah Irving; and to think that home, after all, was sometimes tedious, if a man had to be tied down to it.

It was not always of Margaret that he dreamed

when her fair head slumbered peacefully upon his pillow. He brooded over the dangerous temptation until he grew restless and dissatisfied. Upon every side he was met with evil examples dressed in the fascinating garb of religion; and the object of his passion, herself a convert to the faith, adoring him, waiting for him to ask her love.

Under the influence of a maddening passion, and his own wife, for the time, distasteful to him, he was at last only withheld by the fear of making her wretched. He loved her all the time better than any thing in the world, but just as an intoxicated man becomes a brute and strikes his wife to the earth, to repent of it in his sober hours, he meditated a blow upon her heart. He shrank even while he plotted it, and to escape reflection, rushed into the presence of his bewildering charmer, instead of shielding himself with his wife and child.

One evening he went to Sarah Irving's; it was the third time that week. She evidently waited for him. Her hair was arranged with peculiar taste and she wore a new dress, the materials for which she had brought with her from the east; a black velvet, the loose sleeves lined with crimson, and corals upon her neck and arms. She met him with a brilliant blush and smiles.

"You look magnificent enough for some eastern court," he said, gazing upon her in undisguised admiration, for he had a womanish love of fine array. "Why do you trouble yourself to look beautiful when there are so few to appreciate you?"

"It is only worth while to be beautiful for the sake of one's friends. If I were a wife, I should dress constantly for my husband; when we were to be alone together I would wear my choicest ornaments."

Richard thought of the gentle woman he had left at home, sitting sewing by her little table, in a plain gown of chintz, with a linen collar at the neck. So fair and serene, so neat and unpretending, with such unsullied light in her soft eyes, she was a more loveable image than this brilliant creature before him now, in whose glance triumph struggled over discontent, but he could not see it so then, while blinded by her smile.

"You ought to be a wife, with such views as that," he said; "some man ought to be made supremely happy by your beauty."

"I am in no haste," was the gay reply; "I shall ponder long before I decide who the man shall be for whom I am to trouble myself to be agreeable. You know I have never been very much moved by man's worship."

"I believe that you have treated your lovers rather cavalierly."

"That man will have to vow something deeper than the shallow protestations of the common herd, that wins me to an acknowledgment of his power," she continued, with one of her proud looks.

Now Richard knew well enough in his own thought that with all that indomitable spirit of hers, she had followed him through circumstances which proved her passion much greater than her pride; still, he loved to see her thus haughtily beautiful, and it pleased him to fancy that he would have to beg and plead for her favor.

"But in this common-place age," said he, "how can a knight show any remarkable devotion to his lady-love?"

"There are ways of proving one's devotion."

Carried away by her manner, he slipped down the

precipice upon the brink of which he had so long lingered.

"But I love you, Sarah. How shall I prove it?'

"If you loved me you would marry me."

"I have a wife, Sarah."

"That does not prevent your taking another according to either your belief or mine, or the belief of the community in which we live."

"It does not; but Margaret has not yet been converted to the true belief. What shall I do—oh, what shall I do, Sarah? You are cruel to make me love you thus!"

He had sank upon his knees before her when he first declared his passion; and now he took up her hand from her lap, and pressed it to his lips. His face kindled and his manner was eager and earnest. She withdrew her hand coldly, although she trembled almost perceptibly at his touch.

"You are not fit to talk of love, Richard Wilde —not to me. You are afraid to make a sacrifice. You are afraid of the displeasure of your wife—"

"Not of her displeasure, but her sorrow, Sarah."

'Well, her sorrow, if you choose to have it so. But not of *my* sorrow do you take account. You love me, do you? do you think your meek confession a fit reward for the love which led me to seek your presence through fire and flood? Oh, Richard," she continued in a softened tone, "you know not the meaning of such love as I have given you. Ever since I have been old enough to know the meaning of the term, I have applied it only to you; and long before, the sound of your voice, as you spoke laughingly to me, set my childish heart beating to strange music. I saw you married to another, and felt my own heart turning to stone, and then a fever came after the chill, and I rushed out beneath the terrible storm to cool the fire which rose to my brain. Sternly as I had steeled my thoughts, I fainted when you bid me farewell, to come out here; and when I read the tenets of your religion, supposing you and Margaret converted to them, I left a bridegroom, who waited for me, I left friends and country, and home, and periled life to follow you over a dreary, interminable space, and offer myself to you. You have been my one absorbing thought for years. I have endured wild pangs of jealousy and despair; and in return for this you say, 'I love you, Sarah—how shall I prove it?' You need not

prove it; I will not have milk-and-water in exchange
for the glowing wine which I offer to your lips.   I
would rather complete the martyrdom of myself
which has for so long been going on.   If you were
attracted toward me as inevitably as I have been
toward you, you could not resist your fate—you
would dare and defy all suffering and danger—you
would cry, 'Come to my bosom, *my* Sarah; it asks
you, and it must have you!'"

"I do say so—I implore it! it must be.   I have
thought so long, and now I can hesitate no more.
You shall be my wife—my second wife—but
my most madly adored!   Let us seal our betrothal,
thus."

He attempted to place a kiss upon the mouth
which had just breathed such burning words to him,
but before she yielded, she said—

"You must *swear* to me, first, that you will keep
the engagement; for I scarcely trust you yet."

"Do not distract me with doubts.   I could not
forsake you, if I would; you are too beautiful.
You have been drawing me toward this fulfillment as
inevitably as fate.   But I will swear, if you must
have it so, by all that is holy in earth and heaven,

13

if we both live three months, to make you my wife
There! skeptic, will that do?"

They sealed the unholy promise with a kiss—
sweet, sweet, it may have been, but death lurked at
the bottom of the cup.   The wind arose with a long,
low wail, and swept around the corner of the house,
and rushed away desperately as if intent upon bearing the fatal oath to the unsuspicious ear, which was
waiting to catch the sound of a husband's footstep;
and when it had startled that loving ear, to sweep
on with it up to the sorrowing heavens, and down with
it to laughing hell.   But if the wife's ear caught the
fierce melancholy of the wind's arising voice, it may
have chilled her heart with a nameless foreboding,
but it could not syllable its shriek to the truth, and
it rushed past, over the city, and went crying dole-
fully up and down the plains, and beating itself
against the mountains.

"How the wind rises," murmured Margaret; "the
very sound of it makes me shudder. · Why does
not Richard come back? it's past ten o'clock.   I
wonder what makes me so cowardly this evening.
I will go and sit by Harry's crib; the sight of my
child's face will keep off these nervous fancies."

"How the wind does rage," she sighed, after a time; "what should I do if my husband should die, when he can not be away from me one evening without my feeling so lost and desolate? Darling little Harry; I've a mind to awaken him to keep me company. Eleven o'clock !"

CHAPTER XIII

Thou think'st it much
To mourn the early dead; but there are tears
Heavy with deeper anguish! we endow
Those whom we love, in our fond, passionate blindness,
With power upon our souls too absolute
To be a mortal's trust!

MRS. HEMANS.

It was dark;
When I rose, cold, still, and stark,
It was night; I saw the moon,
And the glow-worms in the grass
Seemed to wonder what I was.

MRS. BROWNING.

"I HAVE got to break the news to her, and I may as well do it first as last," said Richard Wilde in a cold, hard tone, as he approached his dwelling the day succeeding his oath to Sarah Irving.

When a man resolves upon a villainous deed, be sure he will do it in the most villainous manner, for if he should stop to soften it, his resolves may give way altogether; that is, if he is a new beginner.

"I do not see why I should dread it so much," he mused, as he acknowledged the quaking of his heart; "Margaret will be very unreasonable if she

makes any objections. I have been here nearly two
years, now, and have, so far, resisted all invitations to
take another wife; which not many men would have
done. I have been a good husband, and shall continue to be. She shall always have the preference
as my first wife. She need not feel insulted by my
choice, either; I have selected a person with whom
she can associate; her best friend, so that they may
get along peaceably together. My friends are determined that I shall marry again, and I know they
are holding back the office I want, until they are
convinced that I am going to fulfill their wishes. I
have promised them, and I shall not let a woman's
jealous tears stand in the way. I do not see why I
fear anger. She has never spoken harshly to me
since we were married; it is not in her nature. I
do not exactly think I shall like the look of her
eyes; so astonished! but it will be over soon—and
it *must* be got over, that 's all!"

With a look of dogged resolution he entered the
house.

The doors were standing open, for it was a pleasant day, although early in March. Tea waited upon
the table, and little Harry, with his hair brushed

14

into its prettiest curls, and one of his nicest frocks on, ran to meet him as he entered.

He took the little fellow in his arms a moment.

"Where's mamma?"

Henry pointed his dimpled finger toward the garden; and, looking out, he saw her bending over something which seemed to claim her attention.

"It must be done," he said, as he sat the child down.

He stepped out upon the walk.

"Oh, Richard, come here!" cried Margaret, as she perceived him, "these violets are out already. The snow's but just melted away, and here they are, peeping out of the young grass so beautifully."

Her face was all in a glow of delight; for she had a lovely woman's pleasure in things fair and innocent.

"Why, what a fuss to make about a flower," he replied, but he took the one she gave him and played with it in an embarrassed manner.

"It makes me *so* happy to see the spring again. The winter was so dreary; do n't you think so, Richard?"

She put her hand upon his shoulder and smiled in his face; a bright, child-like smile.

"Next week we will transplant those roses and wild-pinks from the plains into the garden," she continued.

"I am afraid I shall not be at home next week."

"Why, where can you be going, Richard, when there's no place out of the city for you to go to? I hope you have not got to go on any expedition among the Indians."

"No, not that."

"It seems as if I could not let you go, even for a day, my husband. You grow more necessary to me every hour."

She put her arms about his waist, and leaned her head against him, as if she thought of losing him for a time, made her cling the more closely to him now. The touch of that brow upon his bosom ought to have consumed its purpose to ashes, but the heart beneath had steeled itself in selfishness until it scarcely quivered even then.

"The truth is, Maggie, I have had a vision. It has been revealed to me what I must do. But before I tell you, you must promise me to be reconciled to the will of the Lord, as revealed by the Spirit to me."

"What can it be, Richard, that is to take you away? If it is any foolish enterprise among the Indians, or in search of further possessions for this people, I do not know that I can promise to be reconciled; not to any thing that places you in any danger."

"What a foolish child you are, Margaret; and a little wicked, too. You speak as lightly as if a revelation was a thing which we could obey or not, as we choose."

The wife was about to speak, but he went on:

"Those to whom the Spirit reveals itself must follow its dictates or forever be cast into hell. I have had a vision, in which it has been told me that I should love you forever, and that we should never die, but live together and see the thousand years of Christ's reign upon the earth, and be by Him rewarded for our obedience and willingness now to cast aside our selfish human will, and sacrifice to Him."

"I have no fault to find with such a vision as that," raising her eyes, laughing and full of love, to gaze in the face of her husband.

There was a moment's silence, while a little bird

went twittering by to its rest, and the sun shot out a lurid ray, from the clouds that rested on the western horizon, which trembled upon the head of Margaret; a breeze fluttered by, sweet with the odors arising from the early flowers; then all was hushed, as if nature held her breath, while the last moment of Margaret's happiness went by.

"And the vision furthermore revealed to me that however against our present temporal wishes, and the selfishness of the flesh it might be, that to carry out all the great principles of our Faith, and attain the mutual happiness to which we now look forward, I must no longer resist the laws laid down, but must take another wife, from among the maidens of the city; and I have thought that Sarah Irving—"

A sharp, low scream, shuddering, prolonged, and strange! who could have dreamed such a sound could ever have been uttered by Margaret's lips that smiled but a moment ago?

"The neighbors will hear you, and a pretty story they will make out of it. Why could you not have listened to reason?" exclaimed Richard, angry at this opposition.

But she heard nothing more of his questions; she had dropped at his feet like a stone, or any senseless thing.

A fear that he had killed her, made the husband tremble; in an agony of remorse he lifted her and carried her into the house.

Their child cried with terror when he saw his mother's strange white face. It was two or three hours before life returned, so that Margaret remembered what had happened, or why she lay there helpless upon her bed. She opened her eyes and saw Richard sitting upon the side of the couch, and became conscious that he was feeling her pulse. She closed them again, she could not bear even the dim lamp-light, and made a feeble effort to withdraw her hand from the one which had clasped her's once at the altar with a vow that was now in ruins.

He attempted to give her some water, but with a sudden effort she put aside the glass and raised herself from the pillow.

"Leave me !" she said, with a faint move of her hand.

He was about to kiss her, to soothe her with caresses, but a look of such mental agony blanched her face, while a fire so vivid leaped to her eye, that he was obliged to obey. He scarcely thought it could be Margaret, sitting there upon the bed with so changed a countenance, with contracted brow and blazing eye compelling him from her presence. Like the wounded lioness the moment before she expires, pain, and a terrible threatening gleamed over her livid face. It was the pride and purity of her injured womanhood, rising up in its self-defense. Love, and the sacred marriage relation, had heretofore sanctified his caresses to her, but now—divorced in heart, and in deed, and word, according to her feeling—the offer of them was mockery and degradation.

He went out, because he found it impossible to do otherwise, and she was alone. She sat there rigidly, looking just as able to sustain herself as a piece of sculptured marble, white and senseless. Her blue eyes were dark and fixed, the lids drooping heavily, and black circles deepening about them.

The candle flared in the wind, throwing fantastic shadows over the walls and around her motionless figure. Her child, when its father went out and closed the door, grew afraid of the darkness and si lence of the parlor, and came pattering softly with his little feet into her room, and took hold of her dress.

"Mamma, mamma," he said, with a grieved cry.

At first she did not hear him, but presently that little voice smote through the anguish which was steeling her heart; a great shudder ran over her limbs and features.

"My God!" she sobbed, "I can not bear the face of my own child;" and she sank back upon her bed, with her face to the wall.

That was the sharpest pang that could by any fate or possibility ever pierce the heart of a woman; she would never know another that was keener than it:—the innocent, sweet face of her own child, bearing in its every feature the reminder that it was *his* child, and so, her own babe, her darling, inflicting agony upon her. *His* child, born of their love —and he alive, and she alive, and this gulf fixed irrevocably between them, and that little grieved face looking up to her in wonder and affright. She did not *think* all this—her brain whirled round and round in a fiery darkness, her eyes were pressed upon her pillow; she was at times conscious of a half formed prayer to die.

Little Harry crept away from the bed into a corner of the room, and laid his head down upon the floor and cried forlornly. A sense of desolation, of being unprotected, was filling his infant heart with fear and grief. He had had no supper, his waiting-maid had gone home to her mother's that evening, and there was no one to care for him. The flickering shadows made him afraid, and his mamma lying there without speaking to him was his worst sorrow. He did not dare to cry very loud; his suppressed sobs echoed piteously through the lonely room; no one came to him to soothe him, to kiss him, and ask him why he was weeping: but infancy has refuges from grief, and by-and-by he cried himself to sleep, and lay upon the hard floor, his cheek pillowed on his hand, and flushed with the tears which had not all dried away when Susan came back and placed him in his crib.

Resenting the manner in which Margaret had dismissed him; resenting even her unhappiness, as if *she* had been inflicting some kind of selfishness upon *him*, with the unreasonableness which always characterizes the offending party, Richard went out of the house in an angry mood. Being angry with himself and stricken with remorse, he chose to believe that somebody else was in the wrong, and that it was only stubborn opposition to his lawful wishes where he had expected obedience, which made him feel so uncomfortable. At first he thought he would go to a meeting of the councilmen down in the city, but he was too deeply disturbed for his pleasure, and he sought consolation where it was most likely to be found. A rapid walk dissipated some of his passion, but it was still with an agitated face that he knocked at Miss Irving's door.

Her little servant-girl ushered him into her presence. She stood to receive him, eager, expectant, with a flush upon her cheek and sparkle in her eye.

" What is it that disturbed you, Richard ?" she asked in her tenderest voice, as she took his hand and looked up sweetly into his countenance.

" The worst is over, Sarah," he replied ; " I have told Margaret."

For an instant the girl was moved with feeling for another besides herself; her cheek paled, and her eyes sought the floor.

"What did she say? was she very unwilling?" she asked when she had summoned confidence.

"No matter what she said, now, my beautiful; I am a little nervous and out of temper, but the sight of you will soothe me, if any thing earthly can. Get your guitar and sing to me your most passionate love-song, Sarah, for next week we will be married; you will be mine—all mine, so soon!" and he flung his arm about her and drew her toward him, while he gazed upon her glorious beauty with a glance of fire.

And the deluded girl was willing to accept this passion, which rushed over every holy thing on earth to attain her, as the love upon which her hopes of happiness were founded. She returned his gaze for an instant with one as warm, and then the lashes swept down to her cheeks, while a blush overspread them which would have been beautiful had she possessed any true title to his devotion.

She shrank away from him and took up her guitar. All that evening she played and sang, laughed and talked, and made herself irresistibly attractive, and Richard reclined upon the sofa, and permitted her to fascinate him. Remorse knocked loudly at his heart, but he laughed the more gayly, and would not hear.   A vision of his home rose up before him, melancholy as a stranded ship gone to pieces on a lonely shore, but he chased it away with the light of Sarah's eyes.

When he retured to his dwelling late that night, his boy was sleeping in his crib in their room, but Margaret with her broken heart, was shut up in terrible solitude, in a chamber by herself.

CHAPTER XIV.

But the night grew damp and cold,
  The sullen wind rushed by—
I seemed to be growing gray and old
  Under that leaden sky,
I felt my cheek grow pale
  And its rounded bloom decay:
The wind rushed by with a sullen wail
    Seeming to say,
  "There will come no day!
Wither and waste and die away!"

THERE was a great rush to the temple the Sabbath upon which Sarah Irving was sealed to Richard Wilde. The bride, with her triumphant expression and beautiful features, elicited murmurs of admiration; but a few pale, consumptive-looking women there were among the multitude, quietly wiped away the tears which stole down their sunken cheeks, as they thought of the first wife abandoned in her home. Their own experience in suffering taught them compassion upon her.

The husband returned with his new wife to her own home. She had built and prepared it in antic-

14

ipation of this consummation. In the second story
she had a beautiful room with an arched roof, and
deep, pointed windows, which she had designed herself, and had constructed by a skillful architect.
This was the bridal-chamber. The furniture could
not be very elegant, but she had added to it by
every little feminine device in her power. The first
flowers of spring hung their blushing heads in
every nook. From the windows scenes of beauty
spread away; and Nature, looking the guilty couple
in the face, with her simple and sublime purity of
loveliness, ought to have been a constant rebuke.
The sunshine of spring was upon every thing. Day
after day, as they sat at the windows, idling away
the time in each other's society, they saw the snow
melt off from the mountains, and rich tints, emerald
and pink, creep over the plains. White clouds floated over the deeps of the sky, and light showers
glittered down upon the blooming earth. It was a
fair and proper time for the happiness of a newly-
wedded couple. The air was rich with the perfume
of flowers, and seemed as full of love and delight as
a living breath. Soft winds stole in and played
with the curls of the bride, lifting them from lovely

shoulder and smiling brow, with as gentle a touch as the lover's who sometimes grew jealous of their dallying, and stole the dark tresses away into his own fingers. Sunlight gilded the arches of the roof, and birds went sweeping by upon dizzy wings, warbling wild carols to the blossoms and the breezes; moonlight crept in with subdued radiance and listened to their evening whispers.

They heard at times a wail upon the wind, and saw a shadow lurking behind the sunlight, but they closed their ears except to the music, and shut their eyes except to each others' beauty. If Richard left her but for an hour, his bride felt as if she were losing him—terror and an undefined foreboding took possession of her; and she ran to meet him upon his return with an expression of joy which would have flattered any man.

She trusted to her great beauty to retain the prize she had won, for despite her theory of passionate attractions she felt in her soul that such attractions were not everlasting; that decay and death were in their very nature. All the time when he was not with her she studied how to render herself more beautiful to him when he should come; what new charm to wind about him, soft and firm like a silken thread.

And yet they knew, this new-married couple, that they were not perfectly happy. A sense of unsubstantiability beset them. Like those who quaff the glowing wine and know that the pleasure it kindles is fleeting and to be repaid with pain, they only drank the deeper of the maddening draughts of their love. If one could have watched them, when they were thus happy together, a shade, a sudden look of pain, might often have been seen stealing upon one face or the other; then its companion would look doubtfully, inquiringly, and a merrier laugh, a more passionate caress would reassure them.

And Margaret! we might leave a blank here upon these pages, as emblems of the weeks that came to her, as far as outward circumstances revealed any thing.

Her life was blank enough; dark as the darkest night that ever settled upon the world, but she had not yet the deadness of desolation which she desired. Flakes of fire drifted slowly and continuously down through the gloom which they could not illuminate, and settled upon her soul. For days she tasted no food and took no sleep. One or two of her friends came in to offer her sympathy; but they went away without speaking a word upon the subject, awed by her marble face.

Neighbors, inquisitive and mean, haunted her house with prying eyes, but she heeded them no more than as if they had been shadows. She said "yes" and "no" sometimes when she was addressed, but there was no meaning in the words.

"La! poor soul, she's going crazy, I believe," whispered one to another, as they left her house.

"She need n't have taken it so hard. All the rest of us, pretty much, have had to get used to it, and so will she."

"If she don't go mad first," replied the other.

"What if she should do as that woman did over in the east part of the city last week?" continued her companion.

"How was that?"

"La! have n't you heard? They were poor folks, rather; lived over there in one of those little houses; but I s'pose she was one of the pining kind Her husband took another wife, a few weeks ago;

15

she did n't make any complaint, and nobody knew she felt so very bad, but one day one of the neighbors just stepped in, when she was alone, and found her hanging from the rafters by a rope, and her little baby on the floor clinging to her dress, and crying. She had hung herself."

" For mercy's sake !" and for a moment there was a thoughtful silence between the two gossips.

That suicide had been committed and a little babe left motherless, clinging to the garments of the dead, touched even their hearts. They were women, although they were degraded ; degraded by circumstances which deprived them of self-respet and personal dignity, and so, of course, hardened their natures, and corrupted what should have been most sacred, ennobling and elevating. Perhaps this quiet tragedy reminded them of the long ago, *when they* should have hurled indignation at the man who had dared thus to trample the heart of a woman under his foot.

All, like these two, had their remarks to make, and opinions to pass; and by far the greater majority of the men and women of the community spoke bitterly and blamefully of Margaret. Her pallid face was a reproach to them, and they could not bear it.

So they turned and heaped honors upon Richard Wilde, commended, admired him, and gave him the position among them after which he thirsted; filled up his cup of glory to the brim; and cursed his wife, in her mute, uncomplaining misery; after the fashion of human nature, generally, when " wise in its own conceit."

When Margaret first began to arouse out of the stupor which had held her faculties in a merciful thrall, the sharp sense of her desolation pressed her so fiercely upon every side that suicide for a time seemed the only relief.

She had always been a religious woman, and had ever strengthened herself to meet calamity with the armor of her faith. She had oftentimes pondered the question: " How could she continue to live if Richard should be taken from her by death ?" and had felt such faith in the durability and purity of their affection, and that their parting could only be for time, not for eternity, that she had schooled herself to endure the loss if necessary, with the patience of a Christian, trusting in God, doing her duty to her child, and holding herself ready to be again united to him when it should please the good Father also to summon her. This was the greatest sorrow her fears had ever conjured up; and now, the blow fell so suddenly, it struck her down, even from her confidence in the love and justice of the Almighty.

There was no resting-place for her tumultuous thoughts. Her child, which had been so unspeakable a joy and blessing, seemed now only to remind her of the brightness which glared from the past over the darkness of the future. She put him away from her. Her girl had almost the sole charge of him; she had not kissed him since the fatal night on which the star of her life went out of its heaven. Her friend—*her friend*—Sarah Irving, and Richard in her company, whiling away in voluptuous happiness, those hours which dragged like the car of Juggernaut over her—of them she could not think, not a moment; and yet they kept flitting before her imagination, tricked out in smiles and beauty, until her burning brain whirled round with a torturing hum, and her heart fainted and lay like a lump of ice in her bosom.

One bright afternoon she put on her bonnet and

vail, and left the house, for the first time since her loss; she had not determined upon any particular direction, but felt that she must walk out in the open air, or the four walls of her room would close in upon her, and crush her brain. She was afraid of madness, and resolved that death should come first.

Her purpose, not clearly developed, and yet tenaciously fixed upon her mind, was to walk rapidly until she came to some body of water deep enough, and there drown herself.

With a hasty step, which was more a stride than her usual graceful and gentle gait, she passed the streets of the city and went out into the solitude. As soon as she was away from the city, she tore the vail from her face and breathed deep inspirations of the pure, wild air.

Almost unconsciously she wandered toward the lake; on and on, hurriedly, over miles of ground, feeling no fatigue. Her feet pressed down the rarest flowers, which gave back perfume, though they were crushed to death (poor Margaret! she could not emulate the flowers, and die with a blessing on her lips; she only prayed silently and fast, for their insensibility to suffering); the blue sky looked down with a calm pity and a sublime love upon her pallid cheeks and hollow eyes; the breeze condoled with her, the meadow-lark sang to her; her mother earth greeted her with such quiet, unobtrusive, and yet evident sympathy, that, for the first time, her overwrought nerves relaxed their tension so that the great tears rolled one after another unheeded from her eyes.

She had gone a long, long ways. The lake was before her, glittering in the light and murmuring on the strand. It was a wild and solitary spot, and very beautiful, where she stayed her footsteps and sat down upon a stone. A rock rose up beside her and partially screened her from the sight of any who might chance to pass along the path which wound by that way, although she feared and thought little of intrusion. She took off her bonnet and bared her brow, which was hot, though livid, to the breeze. The waters looked cooling and she bathed her face in them; she thirsted, but she could not quench her thirst with them, for they would have been to her lips as the waters of life had been, brackish and burning. She looked longingly down into their depths. As soon as she could summon strength to arise from her seat, she intended to try them and find if the peace and rest which they promised from this world's dreadful warfare, lurked beneath them. In the mean time, she sat without any clearly defined wish; memories of her child came to her, but gave her no consolation; faint, far away thoughts of her mother and her New England home, which only tortured her in contrast with the present; a dream, distant and seeming apart from her own experience, of a couple who stood in a dim, sweet-scented parlor and took each other by the hand and promised to love until death, while suddenly the thunder crashed down and broke off their trembling words.

Thus she sat motionless, gazing upon the beckoning lake. She would not have heard the clatter of horses' feet as they swept past very near to her, had not a voice whose lightest tone had never failed to thrill her heart, spoken, and almost by her side.

"Dear Sarah! is not this a beautiful spot?"

"Oh, yes! and I am enjoying my ride so much."

Margaret looked out of her retreat. There they went, flying like the wind, on their handsome steeds, proud, happy, brilliant. Sarah's riding-dress streamed on the wind, but not so gracefully as her dark hair. Her crimson scarf fluttered joyfully; she turned her proud, beautiful head toward her companion who leaned toward her lovingly as he spoke some low, soft word. Away! over the flowery plains rode *the bridegroom, and his bride.* And nature shone just as goldenly upon them as upon the deserted wife; and even the sympathy of nature became a mockery. She strained her heavy eyes to look after them, until they lessened, like two mated birds, out of sight, across the prairie.

She arose to go toward the lake, but all was dark before her, and she wandered in an opposite direction, forgetful of her purpose.

"Will I never reach it? will I never get to the cool water which is forever to quench this pain?" she cried, as she staggered on, yet ever away from what she sought.

Night came and found her still out beneath the starry sky, fainting and ill, but coming somewhat to her sense and sight, and with her feet turned homeward.

What fate was that which would not let her have peace, but which led her steps through that very

street, where the two that had wronged her, found
luxurious refuge from thoughts of her?   She passed
by on the opposite side of the way, and chancing to
look up where a bright light shone from a window,
she had a glimpse of shining arches and gay flowers,
of a beautiful creature bending over her guitar,
whose soft melodies mingled with her impassioned
voice, and behind her, leaning over her chair, in a
rapt and tender attitude, was the man she had come
thousands of miles to rob from his true wife.

The gentleness so peculiarly her own, was all
gone from Margaret now.   She darted across the
street and into the lower rooms without waiting for
permission to enter, found the staircase, she knew
not how, burst open the door of their apartment
and confronted them.   The soft brown curls which
were wont to shade her face, had been knotted up
behind, so that there was nothing to soften the awful severity of her expression; her cheeks had a
round, red spot upon them; her eyes shot glances
of fire.   Sarah dropped her guitar as she sprang to
her feet, and stood faltering beneath that glance;
Richard, too, for a moment, absolutely cowered before the woman he had injured.

"Sarah Irving!" cried the intruder, in a clear and thrilling tone, "I have called you friend for many years; now, shall I curse you with a curse that will ring through eternity, for this proof of your friendship?"

"No; oh, do not!" answered the girl, whose haughty spirit was for a moment quelled by the consciousness of guilt.

"Then give me back my husband. Richard Wilde, you will come away from her, before I curse or kill her."

Awed by her manner, he moved toward the door, but Sarah called out in a voice of agonized entreaty —"Richard!"

He paused between the two. Margaret's eyes took on a wilder look; the light began to flare fitfully, in their sockets; the spirit within was shaken by a mighty storm.

"Did I tell you to come home?" she asked with a laugh; "did I call you my husband? well, I had forgotten! You shall keep him, Sarah; I always knew that Harry loved you, darling; and now you are going to be kind to him. It's all right," with another hysterical laugh, "and now I must go. Richard will wonder why I stay so long; he does not like that I should be away from him much."

She turned with a bewildered air, and fell in taking the first step.   When they raised her she was unconscious of who they were who held her.

CHAPTER XV.

But there rings on a sudden, a passionate cry,
There is some one dying or dead,
And a sullen thunder is rolled;
For a tumult shakes the city,
And I wake, my dream is fled;
In the shuddering dawn, behold,
Without knowledge, without pity,
By the curtains of my bed
That abiding phantom cold.

TENNYSON.

THE result of Margaret's over-excitement was brain-fever. Richard carried her to her own house that night, and summoned a physician to her bed-side. He was not heartless enough to leave her to the care of a servant, or the neighbors. He had not intended by taking another wife to cast the old one away; he had expected Margaret always to occupy the most honorable position, as his first wife, had not her different idea of the marriage relation caused her to refuse the station assigned her. Remorse and affection blended, made him very unhappy, as he kept his solitary watches at her couch.

Sarah now suffered from loneliness; and in her

neglected, weary hours, when she listened in vain for the footstep she loved, she began to realize how impossible it was that a man should devote himself to two wives at the same time. In the madness of passion, when she resolved to run all risks of happiness, in the attainment of her wishes, she thought always to keep the attentions which her beauty and youth had won her.

But as day after day passed, and Richard came not once to ask after her welfare, her proud and passionate spirit chafed itself wild against the bars of its prison. She recklessly wished, that if Margaret could not speedily be well, she would die, and leave her lover to her arms again.

After four or five days he came; she sprang down the steps to meet him, but her warm greeting was received with sadness and coldness. Margaret was no better; but a neighbor had insisted upon watching by her side, until his return; he expected his beloved wife would die; there was reproach in his tone as he spoke, which cut the soul of his listener; but she had coveted her fate, and she would not yield to repentance thus soon.

She did not dare to express her thought that he

15

might leave the sick woman to the care of others and return to her; but she pitied him, because he was pale and worn with watching; she was sure that he needed rest; and she hovered about him paying him every little beguiling attention.

Despite of her kindness he staid but a little while. His thoughts were more with the wasted form upon the bed, in his first home, than with the lovely being before him ; and he went back to keep weary vigils through the night, and have his heart and conscience distracted by what he saw and heard. Margaret was delirious the most of the time, unless she lay in a stupor; and this night her feverish fancies flowed fast from her lips.

Conjured up by her incoherent words, the past, in vivid scenes and processions, glided through the apartment. In the hush of midnight, that low, wild murmur filled the air, and the guilty man sat there trembling and listening. He heard the pebbles crush softly under his tread, when he and Margaret walked upon the shore of the shining ocean, and pledged their love, in the golden days of long ago ; he saw the blush and the drooping eye-lashes, and heard the timid confession, and remembered how his cheek burned as he marked the rose quiver which nestled in her innocent bosom.

He heard his voice, and a lower one, which was that same pure girl's, pledging themselves to each other before the minister; the father and mother looking on, and giving away their darling into his keeping; how had he requited their trust? He saw the bridal-chamber, with its simple snowy curtains, and its perfume of rose-leaves, and that young girl there, his wife, holding his burning heart, hushed in reverent awe, while she knelt in unaffected piety to ask her Heavenly Father to hallow their great love. He saw her giving up all that was dear to her, except him and his love, leaving kindred and country, clinging to him alone, in the hope to make him a religious man, and fully trusting his promises that he would brighten her banishment from home by an increase, if that were possible, of affection, and devotion. He saw her lying pale and faint, but with a smile of the tenderest love and happiness upon her features, as some one placed a tiny beginning of life in his arms, and told him that it was *his* child, and he kissed his Margaret and called her a mother.

He could not bear these memories; nor the tones, now pleading, now sad and reproachful, and anon loving and low, which flowed from those feverish lips in a stream which *would not* cease. He paced back and forth through the gloom, and cursed himself for a traitor, a religious hypocrite, and a murderer. With that same selfishness which had characterized his actions thus far, he could not now, before his accusing conscience, bear his fair share of the blame, but heaped the weight of sin upon the head of his beautiful tempter.

"Human nature could not withstand the influence of that siren creature. She sought me out, with the purpose to tempt me and lead me astray. My church aided her fascinations—my ambition aided both. Sarah Irving! I despise you more bitterly than I can tell; my love is changed to loathing."

So for the present he felt;—so for the present he swore, that if Margaret's life was spared, and his utter repentance could induce her to forgive him, that he would never offend her confidence again.

And to strengthen his resolution he stole out beside the bed where his little boy was forlornly sleeping in unwashed face, and unbrushed curls.

"Poor Harry!" he murmured, "you look like a motherless child, as I am afraid you soon will· be."

And then he sank upon his knees and prayed, partly from révived affection, and more from remorse and cowardice, that the consequences of his sin might be lightened, that the weight of murder might be lifted from his soul, and ·his child not be left an orphan.

As when a beautiful vessel is broken in fragments, the shattered parts still glitter with a melancholy brightness, so in the visions of the sick woman kept drifting and glittering the broken fragments of her happiness. They were never more to be combined, and gradually they floated off into the ocean of the past, leaving a blank and dreary waste. The fever left her brain; and with eyes that· could just bear the faintest glimmer of day, a whispering voice and wasted form, she lay upon her bed, meekly and silently asking to die.

She had not hope enough to infuse strength into her worn frame, and she lay a long time balancing between life and death. Richard was there every day, performing kind services for her, but she asked no questions, receiving what was offered from his

16

hand with the same quiet patience as from the hand
of the nurse. As she observed that he scarcely went
away from the house at all, the thought occurred to
her that he had returned to her with the intention of
going away no more, and for an instant, her broken
heart fluttered as of old; but the fluttering only
gave it pain—in stillness only could it find rest.
She could never again have confidence in him; he
had deserted her once; she could have forgiven him
a momentary infidelity; but this was so deliberately
planned, and so cruelly and selfishly executed, that
her trust was entirely gone.

"I have leaned upon a broken reed. If I repose
upon it again, it will only be to be bruised and fallen
again."

Sometimes he kissed her brow or lips, or pressed
her hand, humbly, imploringly asking her forgiveness in that mute manner. The struggle was great
with her for a while. She would not resist these
little tokens of repentance; she only looked at him
pityingly from the shadowy depths of those hollow,
spiritual eyes. For she did pity him. Her nature
was that of a true woman; she loved him, pitied
him, and at last forgave him. She loved that man—

strange, strange, oh, God! the heart of a woman as Thou hast made it, loving until death, forgiving mortal injury, but true to its innate principles of virtue —she loved him as tenderly as ever, but she felt that she was not his wife; that he had divorced her— that their union was dissolved. Dissolved, but not desecrated. She had been true to him in every deed and thought; she had deemed him as faithful to her; she had seen him go out to meet temptation without even a passing fear for his truth; and now that wedlock was no longer made sacred by one faith, one love, one purpose, it was not wedlock.

Lying there gazing into the world of spirits, whither she expected shortly to go, all worldly passions of resentment or hatred passed away. She felt divine compassion upon the deluded, the ignorant, or the willfully sinful around her; she prayed for the whole of that polluted city, as Christ prayed upon the cross—"Father, forgive them, for they know not what they do."

Now came an incident which aroused her to more feeling than she had thought possible. Little Harry was taken sick. Neglect, and the care of a servant, had been such as to allow him to take a severe cold, resulting in a dangerous fever. She knew how much he must need a mother's care, and she reproached herself that she had so long forgotten him, that she had allowed herself such feelings toward him, innocent, and helpless of his circumstances as he was, and she desired earnestly health enough to be enabled to do her duty by him.

She had his crib brought into her room where she could see that he received proper attention. His moans and feverish tossings distressed her deeply; and the effort she made to get well restored her strength more rapidly than it had been in coming back.

Richard took the most of the care of him. The day that she was strong enough to leave her couch, and creep to his side, her child's illness reached its crisis. Every one thought him to be dying. She sat in her arm-chair and insisted upon holding him in her lap. His little mouth was livid, his cheeks fiery red, and dark circles about his half-closed eyes; while the breath struggled fearfully with the devouring fever which impeded it. Pale, looking more like a spirit than a mortal, the mother clasped him and would allow no one else to take him. At times she wished that death would release him from his agony and then she would have only to follow him out of this desolate world. Again, she only murmured, " 'Thy will be done.' If it please heaven to restore him, I will never again neglect a mother's part."

The physician sat by waiting for the crisis, and Richard knelt before Margaret gazing into that sweet, suffering face of his child. Yes, *his* child, too; and Margaret knew that he had a right to feel the agony which was expressed in his face. In that terrible moment what would not each have given to have been restored to their proper relation? to have felt the mutual sorrow, love, and sympathy which softens the hour of trial? There they sat, separated, father and mother, but not husband and wife, and their child was dying between them.

The joy, the pride they had had in that beautiful boy, the deep, strange fountains of tenderness his coming had unsealed; the mystery, the happiness, and the holiness of the family ties; the light in which he had regarded them before he allowed himself to pervert his belief; his early love for Margaret, his love for her as a mother, swept over Richard Wilde like a tempest.

She saw his agitation, and her slight frame bent trembling over her boy. He yearned to weep upon her bosom.

"Oh, Margaret! oh, Margaret!" he groaned, "my punishment is greater than I can bear. Be recon· ciled to me, or I shall die."

"I am reconciled. I forgive you every thing; I love you as before, but I can never trust you again, Richard."

"Say not so before this dying boy of ours, Margaret."

He leaned his head upon her shoulder, while his form shook like a reed.

"You will be too much for your wife and child both, you must calm yourself," said the physician, approaching and raising him, while he brushed a tear from his eyes. "Let me look at the boy. His breath is easier, there is perspiration upon his fore· head. I think the greatest danger is over. He may get well."

CHAPTER XVI.

I look upon a face as fair
As ever made a lisp of heaven
Faltor amid its music-prayer.

. WILLIS.

Yet, if she were not a cheat,
If Maud were all that she seemed,
And her smile were all that I dreamed,
Then the world were not so bitter
But a smile could make it sweet.

TENNYSON.

HARRY FLETCHER had been a year in San Francisco. He had bent his entire energies to the work before him; he had determined, in bitterness of heart, to be rich—not that he wanted money or expected to enjoy it, but because he wanted some object before him for which to struggle, to prevent his being drawn away into vice or madness. He had succeeded as those usually do who work for a single purpose, turning not to the right hand or the left. The most cunning speculator never had a keener eye for lucky chances than he; and the end of the year found him in possession of the fortune he

strove for. Two hundred thousand dollars well secured and invested, he could count upon as his
own

It was just twelve months since he set foot in that
strange, anomalous city; and this afternoon, as he
walked back from his business to his boarding-house,
a feeling of loneliness came over him, for the first
time. He was home-sick; he would like to see his
mother, and his friends. He asked himself if there
was another, whom he would like to meet; if it was
for *her* this dreary feeling came over him? and he
answered himself, "no!" He had got up a counter-
excitement, and worked a cure; he was himself
again; he could return proud and self-possessed.

From the moment of Sarah's flight, he knew well
enough where she had gone, and for what purpose;
but he had too much confidence in his brother-in-
law to fear for his sister's welfare; and he only
smiled scornfully to himself at the thought of the
folly of the infatuated girl. His respect for her vanished, and his love with it, leaving "an aching void"
which it had taken all this year of labor and excitement to fill; and it was not filled now, but that a
dull, uneasy sense of loss was there.

As Harry walked along the street, taking the middle of it, and grasping a revolver in his hand to defend himself from the danger which lurked every where, and reflected that a year had passed in this unprofitable way—unprofitable to the spirit, not to the purse—his first home-sickness attacked him. He could not keep that away with fire-arms, as he did pickpockets; and it took a very firm hold of him. He reproached himself for not going back to cheer his parents, left so afflicted and alone. All the care of the farm was upon his father, who was growing feeble; and his mother must feel very melancholy, sitting by her little stand, knitting, knitting away in solitude, with the piano never open, and neither of her older children about to amuse, or assist her.

As this picture came up vividly to his fancy, the tears rushed into his eyes; and he felt that his heart was not hardened; that it had come out of the ordeal the same hopeful, generous, and affectionate heart as before; sadder, calmer, not quite so confiding, but not ruined, by any means.

He longed for quiet, as earnestly as he had hitherto for the opposite. The city, with its strangely mingled crowds, its complicated business, its lawless habits, grew disgusting to him; he wished for peace, and the sight of lovely, refined women.

Suddenly he remembered that it was the time for the post-office to be opened; there had a mail arrived, and the distribution was to take place at about five o'clock; there might be a letter from home, or from Margaret.

Dear Margaret! he had not heard from her in months; not directly from her since he came away.

Tender memories of their childhood thronged about him; she seemed to him, too, to be in some kind of trouble, to need him, to call him; and he half resolved, before he reached the office, that he would go home the overland route, and stop at the Salt Lake city to make her a visit. He would carry them a little portion of his wealth; and perhaps Richard would spare his wife for that promised visit home, seeing that she could have such good protection. Sarah Irving might be there where he should meet her, or she might not, he did not care. His heart beat so warmly with these new plans that he was hardly disappointed when he learned that there was no letter for him.

Returning to his boarding-house, he saw, as he passed the windows, a pale, beautiful face, looking out from one of them. He would hardly have been more startled to have seen an angel than a face like that in the city of San Francisco. It was the countenance of a very young girl, pure and innocent as a child's, yet with an anxious expression of doubt and sorrow. He had but a glimpse of it; it seemed to him very exquisitely lovely, set in a halo of golden hair. It looked out upon him from the window of a private room, and as it did not appear at the tea-table, he had no means of gratifying his curiosity further with regard to it. The room in which he had seen it was the one adjoining his own. That evening as he sat close to the thin partition, reading the last New York paper, his attention was distracted by the sound of the suppressed weeping and sobbing of some female.

At last it ceased and a soft murmur reached his ear from a voice so sweet, that he knew instantly to whom it must belong.

"Oh, our Father who art in Heaven, take care of a poor orphan child left alone in this strange, wicked city."

Harry dashed his paper on the floor. For a while he sat irresolute; but the conviction was strong within him that some one needed assistance or protection. He knew very well what a place that city was for the timid and helpless; and that young face he had seen at the window, wore a look of trouble and loneliness.

Trusting to his own good intentions that he should not be repulsed, he left his room, and knocked at the adjoining door. After a little hesitation, it was unclosed, revealing a young girl, standing timidly within, looking at him wistfully, but not daring to bid him enter.

"You seemed to be in distress," he said in his gentlest tone. "I was afraid that you needed a friend, and I hoped that you would not doubt me, when I said that I was just as willing to protect and help you as if you were my sister."

The light shone full upon his frank and kindly countenance.

"Oh! I do indeed need a friend," she said, gazing upon him half hopefully, half with fear, "I am quite alone."

The last words were said with such sadness, and

touching confidence, that all the honor and chivalry of the young man's nature flamed up in his breast; he would have died in defense of this innocent young creature.

"May I not come in a moment, till I see how I can serve you? How came you alone?"

"My father died on ship-board; I had no other friend with me. The ship arrived to-day, and the captain brought me here. Oh, what am I to do?"

"Poor child! were you coming to California?"

"Yes. My mother died long ago; and my father has been wanting to come here for a long time. He was my only relative, and I would not let him leave me. I told him that if he went, I too should go. He did not wish me to come, but at last he consented; and oh, sir, he was ill upon the ocean, and died, and I am all alone."

The very sound of the word "alone" as she said it, seemed to frighten her, there in that strange and wild country.

"Poor child!" he called her again, "you shall not be left uncared for. I am going back to the States in about two weeks; and if you will put yourself

16

under my protection, I will see that you get safely back to the place you came from."

Her large blue eyes opened with a gleam of hope.

" But I know not if I have any money to take me back," she said, the next moment. " If my father had any, I can not find it; I believe that it was robbed from him."

" There are always wretches ready to rob the dead and the orphans," said Harry, indignantly. " But that shall not trouble you an instant, child. I have made two hundred thousand dollars in this city, and I certainly did not make all for my own pleasure. You shall have enough of it to take you back, and to supply your wants as long as you live."

She smiled through her tears, a sweet, sparkling smile, the very pledge of her goodness and innocence. He had taken a curious pleasure in calling her a child, though she might have been seventeen, very small and fairy-like. Now, as she looked up at him, with a grateful, animated look, her little, rosy mouth parted, and dimpling at the corners, and her fair hair breaking in shining ringlets all about her cheeks and neck, he thought he had never met any thing quite so beautiful—quite so perfect a combination of the woman and the child.

"You are so very kind—so very good, I can never thank you, sir," she said.

"Yes, you can. By telling me your name."

"It is Minnie, sir ; Minnie Gray."

"Where did you live?"

"We lived in a little place near New York. My father had a nice old-fashioned house, and a flower-garden around it, but he sold it to get money to come here. Alas! I shall have no home when I return—nor any father," she added, with a sudden burst of grief.

"But I will buy you a home, Minnie."

"You can not buy me friends," she sobbed.

'Oh, yes, I can, plenty of them; but I will not answer for their worth. Are you sure there is no one there who loves you, or whom you love?"

"No one but the minister," she replied, sadly, "and he is an old, feeble man, and will soon die, too."

A suspicion born of his past experience had crept into his mind ; something, he surely knew not what, made the idea painful to him, of taking this young creature to her home and there finding some young man to thank him for it.

"Then you have no uncle or brother—or lover, Minnie?"

"Lover?" she asked, with the wondering look of a child; then remembering that she had read of lovers, and sometimes thought of them, she blushed and said, "Oh, no!"

"Well, I believe you, and I am glad of it. I will not keep you from your rest any longer. Lock your door, and go to bed, and sleep sweetly with the assurance that you have a friend near. If any thing disturbs or frightens you, you have but to speak out loud for me. My name is Harry Fletcher. I will protect you as carefully as your father would have done. Good-night, Minnie."

"Good-night, sir. Is it not strange that God heard my prayer as soon as uttered, and sent you here to be my friend? My pastor taught me to trust to Him when I was in trouble. Good-night."

Harry went to his bed with that simple question of the trusting girl ringing in his ears.

"Oh, why have not men such love, such faith?"

murmured he. " She is as good as she is beautiful. Sweet child! I wanted to take her in my arms and bless her. A timid, lost bird, alighted in this uncongenial clime!"

It had been so long a time since any gentle emotion had disturbed his heart that he could not fall asleep very readily. He lay quarreling with his own good impulses—offended with himself because he found himself still ready to believe that simplicity and truth were yet in the world. As fast as he tried to arm himself with coldness and skepticism, the soft voice of that young orphan in prayer, her clear blue eyes, and childish confidence, stole upon him unawares and left him defenseless before their mystic power.

" Minnie Gray, Minnie Gray! a pretty name to speak, and a very fit name for her. How unlike Sarah she is—small, timid, fair-browed, and fair-haired—it would be impossible for her to do a bold thing. But probably she is a little simpleton, as ignorant as she is innocent—a baby, nothing but a baby. Well, she needs a mother then, of course, and I will take her home with me, and give her to mother, to take the place of Margaret. They will

17

all love her, at home; she is so gentle—she appeals to one's affections so, with her trustful manner and sweet face. She can go to school, if she wishes.

"Ha! it will be amusing for a confirmed bachelor to adopt a little girl, *almost* a young lady; but mother will have the responsibility; and poor Minnie wants somebody to love!"

"Wants somebody to love," the young man repeats to himself drowsily, as he sinks into dreams.

The captain of the steamboat in which Minnie Gray came, had brought her to this boarding-house because there were one or two women connected with the establishment, who might afford her some protection if they chose. What she was to do he was too busy to think or care about; he had done his duty by her, and if he remembered her forlorn situation at all, it was to conclude that so pretty a girl would not remain long unmarried where pretty girls were so few.

The females in the house were of a coarse order; but Harry had made a warm friend of one of them, and to her he went the next morning, and stated the lonely situation of the young girl, and the care he wished taken of her, until he was ready to take her back home with him. The woman promised to treat her like a daughter, and had her occupy the room adjoining her own; so that Minnie, had it not been for her grief at the loss of her father, would have had nothing to trouble her heart about.

She was not deficient in gratitude. She always sat with sparkling eyes, and flushing cheeks, when she heard his step; and in his presence the cloud of sadness which shaded her face, always melted away.

The two weeks, the end of which he had fixed for his departure, passed rapidly. A difficulty arose before Harry which he hardly knew how to settle. He wished to accompany his protegée home by the easiest and swiftest route; he did not wish to send her over the ocean alone; and yet he felt every day, more and more, that he must return by the overland way, and see Margaret. His sister had always been very dear to him; they had grown up together so nearly of an age, that their feelings and sympathies had been in unison; and now, having been from her so long, some deep feeling of tenderness moved him to go and see her. If he should go home the other way, it might be years before he would meet her; and the desire grew stronger each day; and when he heard that a friend of his with his wife, was going to New York in the same steamer he had wished to send Minnie by, he resolved to place her in their care, and go himself to Utah. When he had formed this plan and learned from his friends that they were quite willing to undertake the charge of Minnie, he came to her room and told her the arrangement he had made, and why he was going himself by the overland route.

"The boat leaves in two days, you said, Mr. Fletcher?"

"Yes, Minnie; will you be ready?"

"Oh, quite ready; I have nothing to do but wait for it. How long did you say it would be before you could arrive at home?"

"A year, at least, I think. But mother will be so glad to have me visit Maggie; and tell her that probably I shall bring her back with me—so that the family can very well spare me another year, with such a hope as that."

His companion had been looking at him earnestly, and now the tears which filled her dark blue eyes brimmed over.

"It will be a great while for me not to see you. And I shall not like to go to your mother's without you to introduce me. Oh, I wish I could go your way."

"But the fatigue will be too much for you, you are so delicate; and the journey is perilous in many ways."

"Not more perilous for me than for you. And indeed, if you are to be in danger, I must go along. What if I should never see you again?"

"Well, what if you never should?" asked Harry, looking intently into those tearful eyes.

She grew pale at the thought, and said mournfully—

"Then I should die, for I could not live without a friend in the world."

"My mother will be your friend. And I shall send my fortune home to New York; and I shall leave the sole weighty responsibility of my papers and checks in your hands; and if I should be lost, you will find a will, and that you are remembered in it."

"Oh, how can you talk so lightly about it?" exclaimed Minnie, sighing. "You know it would break my heart—your mother's I mean, and we should all be so sad."

"I laugh because I expect to stay alive, dear Minnie. I have full as good prospects of getting safely home as you, if the Camanches do not eat me up. I rather enjoy the idea of the journey, its novelty and variety."

"But a year!" sighed she, despairingly.

"Is it so long, little one? a year is not much; and I think you can spend it very profitably. I would like you to go to school—some fine Ladies' School."

"To school?" repeated Minnie, curling her rosy lip, and forgetting her tears for a moment. "Why, Mr. Fletcher, I think I am too old to go to school, and I know enough for a woman."

"*You do?* what do you know, now, my wise little girl?" asked Harry, laughing heartily, and gazing into her flushed face with some curiosity.

"I have studied botany, and geology, and conchology, and a little about birds and fishes, and astronomy, and Latin, with my father, and read all his library."

"Whew! I'm surprised," exclaimed the young

man; and he certainly was; he had not dreamed that any thing but loving thoughts, and pretty, childish fancies, lay inside of that bright little head, crowned with golden curls.

"And Mrs. La Martin taught me French. She used to rent one of our rooms, and I learned to talk with her."

"Go on, little Ulysses, what more?"

"Nothing, except the piano, and housekeeping, and raising flowers."

"Ahem! I beg your pardon, Miss Gray. It is I who must go to school, before you will look upon me as a suitable companion; Latin! you look like it!"

'Do n't call me Miss Gray," said Minnie, and the grieved lip betokened the approach of another April shower from the eyes, "and do n't ridicule me; why do I not look like Latin, as you say, if my father pleased to learn it to me? We had nothing to do but study; and I sang to him, and played, and we planted flowers. I am not half so delicate as I look. You know that consumptive lady that came across the country for her health? she could just walk to the carriage when she left her home, and when she arrived here, she was almost well; and I am sure it will do me good to go. You will not think me such a very little girl then, when you see how brave I will be. *May* I go with you?"

Eager, beautiful little face, lifted up with just the persuasive look that induced her father not to leave her behind, when he resolved to emerge from his study and go on a mineralogical and money-making trip to California.

Harry thought a moment, and tried to think calmly, though his heart beat so loudly that it rather disconcerted his brain. He knew very well, that if he took Minnie the overland route, it must be as his wife. He gazed upon her and felt that it *would* be hard for him to leave her for so long; her artless love and confidence had twined itself round and round his blighted soul until it was all in bloom again; but he did not like the idea of the hardships to which she would be exposed.

"The dangers and the privations are nothing like what they used to be," he mused; "as she says, very fragile females have gone that route for their health; and we can take a long rest at Salt Lake City. I think there is a company going sufficiently large that we may anticipate no danger from the Indians."

He looked at her slender form, and tried to feel that it was not strong enough to bear fatigue, but it only appealed to him for protection, seeming to say,

"I am so little and light, you can carry me in your arms, shelter me in your heart. I bloom only in the warmth of love; the ocean breezes will be worse for me, if I am alone, than climbing a mountain would be by the side of somebody who loves me."

"Ah! you are going to consent," exclaimed Minnie, clasping his hand in both of hers. "I see in your eyes that you relent of your cruelty."

"Yes! Minnie, I consent—upon one condition. But perhaps you will think it a very hard one."

"Tell me, tell me! no condition will be too hard."

"That you will become my wife before we leave."

She dropped the hand which she had held so eagerly, and drew back a step, while the warm color rushed up into cheeks and brow. She stood grave and silent, with downcast eyes.

"Well, Minnie?"

There was a world of tenderness in the simple words.

The young man pitied the beautiful embarrassment of the child upon whom he had suddenly thrown the responsibility of womanhood by asking her so weighty a question.

He saw that feelings, deeper than ever before awoke in her young spirit, gave a new dignity to her manner, even while her lip and bosom trembled with their power.

"Your wife, Harry—your wife? it is so sudden."

"But not the less sweet, I hope, dear Minnie. I should have given you a year to think of it. I would not have been so cruel as to make you decide so quickly, and without any mother to appeal to, had you not insisted upon going with me, which gave me hope that you loved me—"

"But I did not mean to—to—"

"I know you did n't, Minnie. Your little head never dreamed of such a thing. But I can not have the privilege of taking care of you through so many vicissitudes unless you give me the best of rights. I am almost afraid to take charge of such a sensitive, dainty little thing as Minnie; yet I will be very thoughtful and gentle with my wife; my fairy wife she shall be, if she will only say the word."

The step which Minnie had receded was taken by her companion, her waist was prisoned by his arm, and as he drew her reluctant head, in its bright and youthful beauty to his bosom, he peeped under the drooping lashes to see if those eyes were not beaming their silent consent.

A very, very happy man, was Harry Fletcher.

"I am glad now, that I am rich, little one," he resumed, after a while, "that I may be able to take just such care of my darling as she deserves. She shall have every thing delicate and beautiful about her gentle way. There can not be any thing too exquisite for her. My mother will be so glad, and I shall be so proud, and every one will love my little wife, because she will love every one. Go now, Minnie, and tell our good friend, Mrs. Smith, that you are to be married to-morrow."

He kissed her and went out, leaving Minnie Gray in complete bewilderment. She sat down to compose her thoughts. Life was full of sunshine and glory to her, but she could not gaze upon all its brightness at once; and the slender hand in which her eyes were hidden, seemed shielding her from too much happiness. Much anxiety, and doubt, and fear, all new and perplexing to her, was mingled with her emotions; it was a long time before she sought Mrs. Smith; and when she did, the good woman, not particularly refined in her feelings, met the burst of tears with which she followed her announcement, with—

"Sakes alive! what are you crying for, baby? do n't you love Mr. Fletcher? he's a nice man, and it's a famous match for a helpless orphan."

"Love him!" said Minnie, while light leaped into her happy eyes, "to be sure I do. But it is so unexpected, Mrs. Smith; oh, I wish I had a mother!"

"Well, child, I do n't wonder. To be sure it's sudden, and I'll help you all I can. Are your things packed?"

The next day Harry Fletcher called the orphan-child his own; he had adopted her, though not in the way he had first proposed.

CHAPTER XVII.

"It may not be—be still, my heart, be still!
 Thou knowest the green fields on the Sabbath shore
Where fountains spring, such depths as thine to fill,
 And where this longing thirst is known no more.
There, on the bursting flowers will fall no blight;
 Music, like that we dream of, fills the air;
There will be morn and glorious noon; but night
 With shadowy wing will never hover there;
   And on the ear
Will fall dear voices that grew silent here."

SARAH IRVING, or Fletcher, as she called herself, sat in her parlor alone one dreary afternoon. The first snow of the season was whirling about in great scattered flakes through the outside air. Her chin was leaned into her hand in her old attitude when thinking. She had been alone in her house two days, and began to feel solitary. She did not know why Richard had not been to see her. Ever since the recovery of his little boy he had been constantly at her house. But she knew that there had been a time when she was in danger of losing him entirely.

The physician, himself the owner of eight wives, although affected at the time by the scene between

17

Margaret and Richard, over their supposed dying boy, thought afterward that the tendency of such things would be bad—would tend to cast discredit upon their creed, and make the wives, generally, more discontented than they were. He waited a week or two, until the child was in a fair way to get well; and then consulted with some of the leading Mormons whether it would not be best to summon the councilmen, and have Richard Wilde reproved, and warned that no heresies would be tolerated.

The consequences were that he was met with public disapproval, and told that no slighting of his second wife, or receding from his avowed principles would be looked upon leniently. His fears were excited. No man ever craved public influence and personal popularity more than Richard; and his ambition urged him on, as it had done at first, to trample down feeling in the race for fame. Besides, he had an interview with Sarah. He had thought to tell her that he could never have any thing more to say to her; he had come to her with some remnants of his indignation against her, still left, but she suspected his purpose, and rendered it impossible for him to fulfill it.

There were tears for his absence and smiles for his coming, and all the influence of magnificent beauty. He had left a broken heart at home, and he could not bring himself to break another here. His situation was not an enviable one. Margaret had forgiven him; had permitted him to share her attentions to her sick child; but she had given him no reason to think that she could ever again become his happy and trusting wife. There was no renewal of old tenderness. All was quiet, peaceable—but a weight was upon the air; an invisible pall hung over the household; and when the child grew well enough to play about, his laugh startled the echoes, a strange, unaccustomed thing.

So, gradually, Richard began to go back to Sarah. It did not surprise or grieve Margaret. She had no hopes. The iron had entered her soul. She had felt from the first the impossibility of renewing the old state of things; she gave up all from the first awful moment when her husband had said—

"I must take another wife."

Since his return to her, Sarah had felt but little uneasiness. She gave herself up to the enjoyment of the life she had chosen, eagerly drinking the wine of the present, looking not back to the past or forward to the future. Richard was her own. The pale woman whom she used to call her friend made no claims upon him; and she shut her heart to the probability that as he had been faithless once he might be twice—that according to his and her belief, he was at liberty to choose as many more companions as he liked. She would allow no anxious thoughts to intrude; yet nevertheless, she seized upon every passing moment with a delirious eagerness of joy, which revealed unconsciously the hidden fear that such happiness must be fleeting. So time sped away and as yet the bitter dregs lay unstirred in the bottom of the cup.

As she sat in her parlor, musing, that snowy afternoon, her thoughts were not much more unclouded than the day. Why had Richard remained away from her so long? She had tried her embroidery, and her guitar in a vain hope to dispel the loneliness which was gathering over her. How terrible it would be, if she should have to spend the whole of the rest of her life in such solitude! all the long, weary years, and she but twenty-two! Perhaps she may have remembered another woman only a year older than she, who had no prospect before her, except the one at which she now shuddered; for she cast away her work with a nervous motion, and commenced walking up and down the room, gazing out with a troubled look every time she passed the window. Was he coming? would the storm keep him away? The snow was, light and dry; he had come to her when the weather was far worse than now. Wearied with watching and walking at last she sat down before the fire and fell to thinking some things not too pleasant. Sometimes the company of the "thoughts of the heart" is not the most desirable, when there are no other companions, and the day is dreary.

As she sat thus, with her face resting in her hand, the sound of coming steps startled her. So, he was coming at last! Her fears vanished instantly; and in their place arose a feminine impulse to treat the laggard coldly, or, at least with seeming indifference to his long delay. She did not spring to the door as usual, to meet him, but sat still while the steps ascended to the door; and then some one knocked, loud and quick, and eagerly, as it were.

"I do believe it is Richard; he wants to surprise

18

me," she murmured to herself as she arose to admit him.

Hastening to the door, and unclosing it, she stood face to face with Harry Fletcher. By his side nestled a little figure wrapped in hood and cloak. A burning blush rushed over the face of Sarah; she stammered as she asked him to come in. Harry extended his hand to her with considerable cordiality; as happy a man as he could afford to be, good friends with every one.

"Why! Miss Irving! I hardly expected to meet you here. This is my wife; Minnie, this is the Miss Irving of whom you have heard me speak."

A little hand was stretched timidly out to her, and a pair of soft blue eyes looked into the dark, proud orbs which returned their gaze for an instant.

"How is Margaret? can I see her this minute? I am so impatient," continued Harry, hastening forward into the parlor, for he was too eager to meet his sister to think of ceremony.

Sarah grew pale as she followed him into the room. "Margaret does not live here. You have made a mistake," she said.

"They told me that this was the residence of Richard Wilde."

"So it is," was the brief reply.

Sarah's spirit had quailed for an instant; but it was indomitable and rose to her assistance again.

"How does that happen?" asked Harry, as a strange fear made his voice tremble.

"He lives here, because this is my house and I am his wife."

"Is Margaret dead?"

He sank into a chair as he asked the question, and Minnie clasped his hand.

There was no reply for an instant.

"How did she die? when? how?" he continued faintly.

"Do not make yourself so miserable, Mr. Fletcher," said Sarah, coldly, though she would have given worlds to have been away from those appealing eyes, "your sister is very well. I suppose that you are well enough acquainted with our customs to know that we think it right and honorable for a man to have more than one wife."

Harry sprang to his feet more quickly than he

had sat down. He towered up so threateningly that the haughty woman involuntarily recoiled.

"I am tempted to *strike* you, Sarah Irving," he muttered between his clenched teeth. "But you are a woman and I spare you. It will be a woeful day for Richard Wilde, though, that brought me to this accursed city. He is a man, or he wears the shape of one, and my sister's cause shall be avenged. Just so certainly as I can meet him, I will kill him. Come away, Minnie, come out of the presence of this concubine! you shall not be sullied by breathing the same air."

He strode out of the door, almost carrying his wife with him; and the next instant Sarah was alone, and not any happier than before this interruption.

The fierce pride of her nature was in arms. Harry Fletcher, the man who used to love her, who had been a suitor for her hand, whom she had deceived and wronged, had spoken sneeringly of her to her face, called her a concubine, and dragged his wife out of her presence as if she were too vile a being for him to endure. She had no way of punishing him for his audacity. She *had* made a con-

cubine of herself; it was disgraceful in his eyes, if
not in the eyes of the community about her, and
her cheeks burned with shame and anger. Her
vanity had received another wound; it was very
evident that her desertion, instead of breaking his
heart, had made him despise her, and that he really
loved that pure, lovely-looking young creature who
clung to him with such affection.

Fear, too, a wild fear! did he not threaten to kill
Richard, if he should find him? his blazing eyes
and determined manner assured her that he was a
dangerous man; that Richard had better take care
of himself. She shuddered at thought of their
meeting.

The snow came down faster, and the wind blew
cold; but after a short deliberation with herself, she
put on her shawl and hood, and hurried down into
the city in search of the man she loved. If she
could see him before Harry met him, she could put
him on his guard. She would beg of him to keep
out of sight for the present, and she would arouse
the jealousy and hatred of the community against
this stranger who came into their midst to find fault
with them, and to put in peril the life of one of

their most esteemed citizens for carrying into practice the commands of the elders and prophets.
She knew that Salt Lake City would soon be too
hot to hold Harry Fletcher, if he dared to express
displeasure at his sister's fate.

In the mean time Harry hurried along forgetful
that his Minnie was tired and that her little feet had
to run to keep up with his huge stride. The first
man he met he stopped to inquire of him the way to
Mrs. Margaret Fletcher's. He had to ask again before he reached the house, for it was a considerable
distance from Sarah's.

"Minnie," he said, as they stood on the step, "I
can hardly summon courage to meet my sister," and
he did look pale and faint.

His anger toward her husband had kept him
from thinking of the anguish of meeting her,
until he was at the door. A little girl answered
their summons, and asked them into the sitting-
room.

He had a glimpse of Margaret before she saw
him. But *was* that Margaret—that almost phantom
form which arose to meet the visitors, with its wasted
cheek, its languid eye and feeble step? *was* that the

stately and blooming woman who left her home in New England but three years ago?

"Margaret! Margaret!"

The cry came up unawares from Harry's heart to his lips.

She gazed at him a moment, and then, answering his cry, she sprang into his arms.

Her head dropped upon his shoulder; he felt that she had fainted, and when he laid her down upon the lounge there was blood upon his coat and upon her lips. Minnie took her head on her lap and her husband brought water.

"Oh, Maggie, what have I done to you, with my sudden coming?" he cried in distress.

Presently she opened her eyes, and smiled at him.

"Do not be alarmed," she whispered presently, "it is often so now-a-days. Any little excitement brings it on; it is not very bad this time; I shall be better quickly."

"Do not speak," said her brother. "Keep perfectly still, and when Minnie and I have taken off our extra clothing and warmed ourselves we will talk to you."

They laid her in an easy position upon the lounge,

where she remained quiet, her eyes half open, fol
lowing every motion of Harry's with a faint smile
in their mournful depths.

He took off Minnie's hood and wrappers, and
placed her by the fire, with her little feet on the fen-
der; for the poor thing was quite chilled by the
storm; and when the roses began to come back to
her cheeks, and she looked like her own pretty self
again, he said to the invalid:

"This is my wife, Margaret; Minnie you must
call her, when you get well enough to speak."

The young wife turned her fair, childish face to
smile upon Margaret, but her tears got the better of
her smile, and the next instant she had her soft cheek
pressed to the pale one of her new sister, and was
whispering in her ear—

"I love you so much. I loved you before I saw
you, because you were Harry's sister, and now, oh,
so much more!"

Then, alarmed lest she should excite. the invalid too much, she caressed her hand a moment, and
retreated to the fire.

A bright-eyed little boy about two years of age
now peeped into the room, and finally ventured to

come quite in. Harry had never heard that his sister had any children, but his heart told him at once that the beautiful child was hers. He took him in his arms, and asked him his name softly.

"Harry," said the little fellow.

"I named him for you," whispered Margaret. "Harry, this is your uncle that I have told you so much about."

"Yes, I am your uncle Harry," said the young man with a trembling voice, "and I am going to be very good to you. You will love me, won't you?"

And with the child in his arms, he hurried into the next room. He was unwilling to distress Margaret by the sight of his agitation. That innocent child, unconscious of the cloud about his future, unconscious of his mother's misery, touched a chord in his soul which vibrated strong and loud. He walked back and forth through the dining-room, still holding him, but the arms shook with which he held him, and his tears fell like rain.

"I will be your father, little one," he said to the wondering infant, "and Minnie shall be your mother. You shall not know what you have lost," and then, as it began to cry from sympathy, he gave it something to amuse it, and let it go, while he sat down and leaned his head upon the table in an agony of grief. He had loved Margaret so; he had been so proud of her beauty and virtue; she had been to him the ideal of true womanhood; she was his only sister; this blow would fall so upon her parents—he was overwhelmed for a time by the might of the storm. It was the return of his indignation against Richard which finally dried his tears.

The grief of a man like Harry Fletcher is terrible to see; and his anger is equally terrible. He never knew before of what passion his nature was capable. He felt that if Richard Wilde was before him, he should strangle him, crush him, and thrust his lifeless body from his sight with fierce contempt. He resolved that his life should atone for this injury.

"He has killed my sister. I could inflict no death upon him so lingering and torturing as this which she is enduring," he muttered.

Love for his sister subdued him when no other thing could have mastered his excitement.

"If she sees me in this furious plight, it will agitate her too much: I must be calm before her;

but my revenge is sure." He calmed himself as far as possible and returned to the parlor. The quick eye of Margaret, having the preternatural sight which belongs often to the sensitive and nervously diseased, detected the resolution which he thought he had put away from view. She beckoned him to the sofa.

" I have forgiven all, and you must do the same," she murmured.

" I can not."

" If you love me, you will, Harry, for my sake. I am so weak I can not bear any thing more, and if you should—"

She paused, but her pleading eyes said more than her pleading voice.

" Well, *for the present*, Maggie, I promise you. But it is hard."

She breathed a sigh of relief and gave him one of her gentle smiles.

After tea, which her servant prepared for them, Margaret was able to sit up in her easy chair, and hear the history of her brother since she parted from him. It was the first she had ever learned of the particulars of Sarah's desertion; he touched upon the matter briefly, and in a way which convinced her that the wound to his heart had healed without a scar, and that the fairy wife, as he called her, who heard him without annoyance, relate this story of his first love, was sure that she now held as secure a place as if this first love had never existed.

"I have made a great fortune, Maggie," Harry concluded, in his old-fashioned, hearty way. "I hardly knew for what purpose at the time; though it has all been made very clear to me since. First came this helpless, dainty creature, who will have to have roses scattered under her feet through life—and roses have to be bought now-a-days with gold—she came and put in her plea for a portion."

"Nay, now—" tried to interrupt Minnie, but he kept on:

"And next here are you, and little Harry. Harry did not take his name to have nothing with it. I am his god-father and shall see that his name is worth something to him.

"My darling sister, you shall go back with me to our old New England home. If father and mother want to live in the old house they shall do so; and we will have one close beside them; otherwise we will build a mansion large enough to hold us all; and we will see if we can not forget, in the midst of luxury and tranquillity, these dark days. We will be happy yet, Maggie."

Her lip quivered.

"I feel that I might enjoy not happiness, but peace perhaps, living with you and your sweet wife, Harry, but I shall never see New England again. My health is gone, and never to be restored. Your kindness will have a chance to work for the good of my child, though; I never can tell you how much relief and joy your coming has been to me. Truly God is good. I should have trusted him more firmly. The thought that little Harry is to be removed out of this polluted atmosphere, that he is to have the benefits of a New England home and education, and that he is to be guarded by your love, will make my death-bed sweet and welcome: I have only lived for him."

"You must live for those who love you now, Maggie—for your father and mother, for me, and for your boy. We will stay with you here until the pleasant spring weather. You must take this win-

18

ter to get well in. Far away from these hateful
associations, you must let memory close over them
like the grave; they shall never be referred to; and
in the society of those who love you so deeply, so
dearly, you will yet have much that is delightful."

"You are a good brother," she replied, with a
melancholy smile; "but you have come too late. I
bore the stroke alone, and I had not strength to resist the effects. Besides, however sheltered I might
be in the bosom of my family, I could not endure
to go back to my old associates under such circumstances."

He saw the pain which contracted her brow, and
avoided the subject for the rest of the evening. His
strange experiences in California life, made an interesting topic, and he exerted himself to beguile
his sister from her sadness. She smiled at his
amusing adventures, and was interested in all, but
there was a heart-broken expression in her smile
which was more touching than her sadness.

Nevertheless she felt a tranquillity which had not
been hers for a long time. She was not so solitary,
so utterly desolate; the house was not so much like
a deserted mansion as it had been. A feeling of

greater happiness than she had thought possible returned to her at the thought that her child was provided for ; and despite the unusual fatigue she had
endured through the day, she slept that night more
undisturbed than she had for many weeks.

When she awoke in the morning, it was not to
the silence and loneliness which usually greeted her.

Little Harry was half wild with pleasure to think
he had found an uncle who was so kind to him
The poor little fellow had been so lonely, with only
his sad mother for company, who did not play with
him as she had once done.

CHAPTER XVIII.

SEVERAL weeks passed away. There was a great change in Margaret's household. She had nothing now to do but to lie upon the sofa, and be an invalid; for Minnie, with a spirit no one would have dreamed her possessed of, had taken the charge of the household matters upon herself. She wanted Margaret, she said, to employ her time in getting well enough to go with them upon the first bright day of spring. There was an air of cheerfulness and life about the house wherever her light footstep trod, or her bird-like voice sounded. She was like sunshine to the shadowed heart of the invalid; she brightened and warmed it; but it had been withered never to bloom again.

Despite their utmost efforts, Margaret faded day by day. A distressing cough wore out her nights, and frequent bleeding at the lungs weakened her yet more rapidly.

She told them that she was not now unhappy: that her earthly hopes had been very suddenly and ruthlessly torn from her, and that for a time she could not be reconciled. She had gone to Christ in her greatest agony, and found that His precepts were to love your enemies and do good to those who despitefully use you! If she could do a kind thing for Richard or Sarah she would do it; but she grieved for their willful selfishness; she pitied them, she forgave them; she did not wish Harry to take up her cause against the man who had once been her husband.

Harry always talked soothingly to her; yet he had very little doubt in his own mind, but that it would be dangerous for Richard to come in his way. As long as his sister desired it so earnestly he would refrain from seeking the recreant, but he could not promise himself that his wrath would not boil over, if they should chance to meet face to face. So far he had seen nothing of him. Richard had not called at the house; and Harry had gone out but little. The people were not disposed to regard him

19

with much favor, and he was sure that his feelings for them were not those of the highest esteem.

One day, when the weather was warmer than usual, the servant-girl was sent to walk with little Harry, and came back without him.

"Why, what have you done with my child?" asked Margaret.

"His father came and spoke to him, and coaxed him away. He told me he would send him back when he got tired of him."

Night came, but not the child. One, two, three days, and Mr. Wilde did not yet seem tired of his boy.

Margaret's anxiety was so great, that it added to her fever and unrest very much.

"Can it be possible, Harry, that he will be so cruel to me as to take my child away from me?"

"Very likely, Maggie. At least, I shall go and see about it. You shall not be kept any longer in suspense. You shall have little Harry in your arms this night."

"Oh, do not be rash or harsh if you go, dear brother. Remember how long it has been since Richard has seen the child, and that he can not come here to visit him. As you are going to take him away so soon, perhaps we are selfish about wanting him back."

"Yes! I will remember," was the bitter reply. "I will remember how selfish you are to want your boy, and how delicate his father must be about coming here to see him."

About the middle of the afternoon Harry started on his errand. He knocked at Sarah Irving's door, and without waiting for any one to answer the summons, he opened it and walked in, just in time to see Sarah pushing the child out into the back room, while Richard advanced to meet him.

"My sister Margaret sent me for her child," said the intruder.

His voice was calm enough, but a suppressed fire burned in his brave and threatening eye.

"Your sister Margaret can not have *my child*," was the sneering answer. "I understand that it is your intention, without my consent or approval, to take him out of this country where I shall never see him again. Now, I have a right to dispose of my own children, and shall submit to no dictation. Besides, my religion teaches me that this city is the

refuge, and will be the abiding-place of the Latter
Day Saints, and I am not willing to see my son
damned by letting him out into the world."

" *Your religion!*" said Harry in a tone of inconceivable scorn, "your religion teaches you that he
must remain in this hell upon earth. I came for the
boy, and I am resolved to have him. You have
outraged the heart of his mother enough already.
Do not dare to provoke me by recalling it too vividly to my memory;" and he strode toward the
door through which he had seen the child dis-
appear.

Richard placed himself before it with the words:

"There was no reason why the child need to have
been separated from his mother, if Margaret had
not played the fool. Go back and tell her that
when she comes to her senses, and rejects all unnecessary advice from relatives, and does as the
other women of this country find it their pride and
duty to do, she will have both her husband and
child, without any trouble."

"It was my sister who played the fool, was it?
well, I will play it over again."

Swift as thought Harry drew a revolver from his

bosom, and fired upon his insulter. He was very quick, but not more quick than the eye of love. Sarah, who was standing near, with an impulse of pure affection, which sanctified somewhat her reckless course, threw herself upon Richard's bosom and received the discharge in one of her lovely arms. She did not scream, but sank down dizzy with the pain and fright. The instant he saw that he had wounded a woman, Harry was filled with regret. He paid no more attention to the man, who did not dare to lift her up, but stood quailing with fear of another attack; his own arms which he usually carried, he had left in his bed-room not half-an-hour before—but rolling the sleeve up from the wound, he examined it with the eye of a person who knew something about surgery.

"That wound is not dangerous, thank God!" said he. "Strange that a woman will risk her life for such a puppy. Bind that up immediately, sir, and go for a surgeon without delay."

Still holding his revolver pointed at Richard, he opened the door, and called little Harry to him, who gladly came, and they retreated from the house together. Richard was obliged to take care of

Sarah, which gave him ample time to reach home safely with his prize.

"This arm will never be beautiful again," murmured Sarah, when her companion had stanched the blood and revived her with some water. "But it ought to be dear to you, Richard, for it saved your life. How glad I am that it could do such service."

That night a furious mob gathered around Margaret's house. The news of the affray had flown like wild-fire, with all the circumstances willfully distorted by Richard Wilde, who gave the impression that his wife Sarah had been coolly shot while defending his child from being kidnapped.

"Hand out the dog! he shall be hung this night!" they shouted. "He is an enemy in the camp! he makes some of our wives discontented, and others he shoots! He shall meet with the same fate he deserves."

The front and back doors were bolted, and they resisted invasion for some time, so that the wretches outside began to cry,

"Burn the house! burn the house over his head!"

And this they might have done, had not Richard

restrained them by cautioning them that his child and wife would also fall victims to this plan.

At last, just as the front door was yielding, it was opened, and Margaret confronted the crowd. Her fragile figure, and ethereal face, showed spiritually in the glare of their torches. Her calm, heavenly countenance, purified by the near approach of death, awed them like that of an angel's.

"What would you do?" she asked in a sweet ringing voice; "if you seek revenge, seek it upon me, for it was I who sent my brother for my child. Do you wonder that a mother should want her child?"

"What has that to do with the shooting of Sarah Irving?" growled a savage voice.

She would have spoken again, but Harry pushed her aside and faced his enemies; his wife, though, stood before him, and her delicate form was his shield. He held a revolver in each hand; there was nothing of the appearance of coward about him, and when he put even his wife away, and stood there undaunted, a murmur of indignant admiration arose at the bravery they hated.

"Come on!" he cried, "I will sell my life at a

high price. A dozen of your lives shall pay for mine. Come on, the first who dare! But let me, before I go further, redeem my memory from the stain of cowardice which would rest upon it, should it be thought that I willfully shot a woman. I did not. It was Richard Wilde, the craven, whom I aimed at, and the woman threw herself between us. He was not worthy of the sacrifice. I went to his house to get for my sister her child. Look upon her! does she look as if the few weeks she has yet to stay in a world which has been too harsh for her, need to be made more miserable by the robbery of her child? Go to. Let it not be said that *you* are murderers—that you came here to her threshhold and killed this feeble woman by your violence. It is not for myself I ask your mercy. I ask no favors. I will take care of myself. If you think this scene of terror and excitement, fit for the endurance of this dying sister, continue it. For my part, I am ready."

"We will withdraw," muttered the mob sullenly. "We do not wish to harm Mrs. Wilde. But you, sir! if you show your face out of doors while you stay here, you will rue it."

CHAPTER XIX.

Oh, there is a sweetness in beauty's close
Like the perfume scenting the withered rose
For a nameless charm around her plays,
And her eyes are kindled with hallowed rays;
And a vail of spotless purity
Has mantled her cheek with its spotless dye,
Like a cloud whereon the queen of night
Has poured her softest, tenderest light.

PERCIVAL.

PAYING no attention to the threats of the people, Harry Fletcher did as he pleased about going among them. Whenever there was any thing wanted for the house, and whenever he and his wife wished to go out for exercise, he did not hesitate to show himself in their midst. The bravery of his demeanor, and the knowledge that he went thoroughly armed, and that any attack upon him would result in the loss of several lives, preserved him from any thing beyond ill looks and muttered words.

He took particular pains to inquire after Sarah. Falsely as she had played the part of friend toward his sister, he was sorry that he had done her personal injury; and was glad to learn that her wound was rapidly healing, with no more serious consequences than a fever, and a few days' confinement to her bed.

The excitement of that day and evening in which she recovered her child, hastened still more the decay of Margaret's health. She seldom sat up more than two hours a day; every exertion, however small, was followed by spitting of blood; her flesh grew more transparent, and her spirit shone through it more luminously, week by week. Harry no longer deceived himself with the thought that she would ever be well; still, he could not help hoping that the warm spring would enable her to be removed toward home. He could not endure the thought of leaving even her grave in that detested city; he wanted her to die in the midst of the friends who had loved her from childhood.

The first sunny days found her unable to leave her bed. It was just a year since her sorrow came upon her; and it may be that the breath of the violets and the soft breezes of spring brought back keener memories of that time, and wore upon her ethereal frame, which could bear nothing more.

Her preparations for death were made. Her child she had given, with no mistrust of the noble affection of her brother, into his keeping. Gifts and messages of love she prepared for her absent family.

One request she had to make of Harry, which touched him deeply. She wanted him to promise that her parents should never know the cause of her death. She wished them to believe that she died happy; that their hearts might never be tried by the knowledge of her sufferings, which it could do them no good to know. That Harry had her boy might be accounted for by saying that it was her wish that he should be taken East for the benefits of education, which could not be given him so fully in Utah.

If Richard could have seen Margaret at this time, the comparison would hardly have been in favor of Sarah. One was gorgeously beautiful as an Indian vase, with the fire and smoke of incense burned before a false god, flickering within; the other was like a snowy and slender vase of the most fragile porcelain, in which some waning star was imprisoned, waiting to escape to its native sky.

"There is a sweetness in woman's decay,
When the light of beauty is fading away."

At last there came a day whose successor was not to find Margaret; her next morning was not of Time but of Eternity.

She had lain speechless for many hours. Harry knew that his earthly hopes for her were over, and sat by her bedside with a despondent face. She unclosed her eyes and whispered to him—" Go for Richard and Sarah. I have a dying request to make of them; tell them I send in love, not in anger."

Harry's proud spirit would have rebelled at this, but he could not disobey those mute, solemn eyes, which pleaded against any objection he had to make.

He left Minnie to keep watch, and hurried out, with a swelling heart, and choking sensation in his throat, resolved to do the message himself, that no accident should prevent its delivery.

Again he knocked at Sarah's door. She opened it herself. If she had been a timid woman she might have started at sight of her visitor; as it was, she stood silently waiting for what he had to say.

"Margaret is dying," said the messenger, and the words sounded hoarse from his lips. "She wishes to see you and Richard, if you will come. She says that she sends, not in anger, but in love—she has a request to make of you."

Sarah stood for a moment undecided.

"We will come," she then answered.

"There is no time to be lost," he said, as he hurried away.

Sarah pressed her hand hard against her heart, as if to keep it from bursting its tenement. That was an awful announcement which had just been made to her—that moment she stood face to face with her guilt.

She was not a woman to shrink from the ordeal before her; she had been very selfish, but she would not slight a dying woman's summons, be the consequences what they might to herself.

She went back to her room.

"Richard, Margaret is dying, and has sent for us."

19

"How can we go?" he questioned her in dismay.

"We *must*," was her brief reply, as she threw on her bonnet and scarf. "Come, no shrinking now."

Fast and silently, they walked along together, their troubled thoughts they kept to themselves, but we may well guess they would hardly care to clothe them in words.

Margaret had not spoken since she gave the message to her brother, until they entered the room. Again she unclosed her eyes, large and bright like a spirit's, and asked Harry to raise her up and hold her head upon his bosom. He sat upon the couch, and supported her in an easy position. Did Richard feel that another occupied the place which should have been his?

Sarah, obeying the look of Margaret's eyes, stood close beside her. She was pale and rigid, but her glance met that of the dying woman earnestly; she was willing at that moment to make any atonement required, or to do any thing which might be asked of her. Some remnants of nobility were yet undefaced in her character.

"Do you love Richard truly and only?" asked Margaret.

Her voice had come back to her; its tones were sweet and solemn.

"I love him truly and only, and beyond all earthly things," was the equally clear and solemn reply.

"And you, Richard, do you love Sarah truly and only?"

She put the question in the same form to him, for she wished to believe the best of him.

"I love her truly," was the almost inaudible reply.

A gleam of pain shot athwart Sarah's brow; what right had she to expect he would say he loved her only?

"I have no reproaches to heap upon either of you," continued Margaret. "I have forgiven you both all the injustice you ever did me; I love you, and would do what is best for both of you. I am Sarah's friend, if she is not mine. Knowing from my own case, all the unhappiness which must come from such a belief as you have acted upon, and trusting that Sarah loves as truly and faithfully as I loved, and wishing to save her what I have suffered, I would only ask you both to remain constant to one another. Will you join hands here before me, and promise to remain true to each other, one husband and one wife, so long as you both live?"

Sarah looked up at Richard eagerly, and half held out her hand to him. He blushed and wavered.

"Is it so great a thing to ask?"

That spiritual glance penetrated his false, unstable soul. He would have been glad to have been a thousand miles away; he tried to call to his aid some of the sophistries of his religion, but they showed so hollow in the clear light of that dying presence, that he felt impelled to tell the whole truth without apology of any kind.

"I would have done it, because you asked, Margaret," he answered, "had it come sooner. But it is too late. I was last week sealed to another wife."

Sarah drew a gasping breath. It was news to her as well as to the others. Margaret looked at her pityingly.

"I am sorry I could not save you this," she said.

Sarah bent over, and whispered something in her

ear, which no one else heard, kissed her cold fingers twice or thrice, looked into her sympathizing eyes with an agonized expression, and went out of the room.

For a short time all was hushed as the sick woman struggled for life, to fulfill the rest of her desire; she conquered her exhaustion and spoke again:

"You will not deny me this, at least. Our boy —I wish to give him to my brother to be brought up away from these practices which you know—I do not—think holy. Oh, let me have my dying wish about him. It may be hard—for you to part from him—but not more hard—than for me. He will be kindly cared—for. Promise me that you will—make no resistance when Harry—attempts to take him with him. Promise me—Richard."

The child sat upon Minnie's lap, looking at the swiftly altering countenance of his mother with startled eyes. His father glanced at him; he was a bright and noble-looking boy who might well arouse a parent's pride. He did not like to give him up. But the heart not faithful to its marital affections can not have even the paternal instincts

20

very strongly developed; and he dared not refuse the last request of the woman he had murdered— ay, murdered—so his soul put the matter to him then. These weak and broken accents had a power too great for his will.

"If it must be so, Margaret, it must. Harry shall have the child. Oh, Margaret forgive me," he cried, with a sudden burst of emotion, sinking upon his knees by the bed.

"I do forgive you, dear Richard. But God forgives—only—those who repent. I have prayed for you. My child—bring me my—child."

Weeping, Minnie held the warm and rosy cheek of her boy to her chilly lips. She kissed him and expired.

Harry laid her gently down, and Minnie folded the hands above the broken heart which was now at rest. Richard kept his position a long time, with his face concealed in the drapery of the couch.

"Shall I go or stay," he asked Harry when he arose.

"I have nothing to do with you," was the cold answer. "It was my sister's wish that I should have no trouble with you, and her wish is more sacred with me than my own sense of right. In her angelic forgiveness lies your safety. She shall not be buried within the limits of this city, nor shall any Mormon priest officiate or any Mormon ceremony desecrate her grave. If you wish to attend her funeral, I shall not forbid you. It will take place to-morrow."

Minnie, whose gentle and loving spirit, had borrowed for the time, some of her husband's resentment toward the people, would permit no hands but her own to assist in adorning the beautiful corpse in its last attire. She smoothed down the flannel whose warm folds could impart no animation to the breast beneath; she arranged the brown curls down either side of the face, as they had been worn in life, and decked them with snow-drops and violets.

Harry went off toward the mountains and found a sheltered nook, where early flowers were blooming, and the sunset light would fall. There the whip-poor-will would trill his lonely dirge, night after night; there the eternal mountains would look down benignantly; there the roses would bloom in June and July, and the brilliant leaves of autumn would drift above the mound.

The next day they brought her and laid her down to her dreamless sleep. "Peace! peace!" murmured Harry over the grave, " thou hast found it, sister, and we will leave thee to thy rest."

There was but Harry and Minnie, Richard, and one or two who had been kind to the dead, who saw where she was laid.

A small gray stone was placed at her head upon which had been hastily carved her name

MARGARET.

CHAPTER XX.

"I have sinned," she said; "man is weak, God is dread,
  But the weakest man dies with his spirit at ease,
  Having poured such love-oil on the Saviour's feet
    As I lavished on these!"

                              MRS. BROWNING.

"Forgive us our trespasses as we forgive those who have trespassed
against us."

THE brief preparations necessary before resuming their journey were soon completed by Harry and his wife. The keepsakes which Margaret had prepared, and a few mementoes which she had bequeathed to her child, with his little wardrobe, were all they took from the house. It was in good order for Richard Wilde to introduce a new wife into, should he desire. They departed in company with a band of returning Californians who had been recruiting for a week or more in Salt Lake City.

The evening after their departure, Sarah went out for a walk. She went alone just after sunset. Richard could not accompany her for he was going to take his new wife over to her mother's to get her clothing, etc., and bring them home. The three had taken tea together—Richard, Sarah, and Harriet, the last comer. The house which Sarah had built with her own money was to be the home of one and all. She had met the new comer haughtily, with a quiet, queenly assumption of superiority, but pleasantly. The pride of her dead father, which had descended to the daughter, instigated her to conceal her feelings, if she had any upon the subject; and all the afternoon she had treated her rival with the courtesy due to a stranger and visitor.

She walked out toward the mountains. It grew dark but she could not bring herself to turn back; if she retraced her steps they would lead her back to her home—that home which she had erected under the influence of a delirious, fanatical passion; and if she should go in, she would find the man she loved enjoying the smiles of another woman, not so beautiful, not so refined as herself.

No, she could not turn back just yet! the moon was at the full, and she hurried on through its ghastly brightness, until suddenly she came to a fresh-heaped mound, with the sods laid carefully over it, and flowers strewn around—the head-stone gleamed in the pallid night with a name she knew too well.

"It is Margaret's grave," she said.

She threw herself prone upon it and buried her feverish face in the damp grass. It might have been an hour in which she did not stir; her garments grew wet with dew; there was no sound except now and then a convulsive sob.

"Oh, my God," she cried after a time, sitting up and lifting a wild face to the moonlight, "my punishment is meet—my repentance is bitter. Margaret! Margaret! why did you forgive me? why did you, upon the death-bed where *I* placed you, make a dying effort for the happiness of the one who blighted yours? you have indeed heaped coals of fire upon my head. Great heaven! what madness! am I the creature who was once an innocent child, who went hand in hand with Margaret to school, who read out of the same book, who wore the same colors, who grew up like a sister by her side? What did she ever do all her life long but forgive me, yield to my will, humor my fancies, love even my faults?—and to reward her for this, I followed her, and stole from her the husband, the father of her child, gloried in her desolation, trampled out the bloom from her life—killed her! Ay, here she lies in her narrow bed, senseless and cold—her heart will never ache again. I would give all the years of this life, and the eternity of the next, had I the power to undo my work—to restore the pulses to the heart which lies there a silent and everlasting reproach. Its silence is more awful than curses; I would that the dead might shriek me some reproach to break the stillness.

"Margaret was so gentle—she was so good—I misunderstood her: I thought she had but little affection because the stream flowed deep and quiet; because it did not foam and dash, like the mountain torrents of my spirit. As if the very nobility with which she overlooked all my follies did not prove a capacity for more Christ-like, immeasurable love! It was for *me* to say that she could live with half the heart of her husband, to take away from her her rights, because I weakly, wickedly, coveted what was not mine.

"You are no true woman, Sarah Irving; you have debased yourself below the level of your sex;

you are ashamed to face your own soul—ashamed
to go back to the people from whence you came, and
you find it impossible to go forward with those you
have chosen. Oh, *what can you do ?"*

She pushed the damp hair back from her cheeks,
and gazed fixedly toward the city.

"They are sitting there, I know, in that room of
mine. Her cheek is upon his breast; he is smiling
into her eyes. Fool that I have been! is it not
good enough for me? Can I feel, with all this
misery of passion and despair, a tenth of the agony
which I ruthlessly heaped upon Margaret!

"Fondle your new possession, Richard Wilde! it
was I, with the eloquence upon which I prided myself, who won you to believe that lust was love—
that infidelity was virtue, and constancy was the
weakness of the cold and stupid.

" It was easy for me, after I had tainted the sweetness of womanhood, by yielding a belief to the philosophy of Socialism, to take the other short step into
Mormonism. The difference is too little for a mind
which has received a downward impetus to stop at.
Whether it be holier for a man to change his wife
with the caprice of passion, or to institute a harem

and have a dozen at the same time, is not much of a question. Whether the doctrines of Stephen Pearl Andrews be better than those of Brigham Young it takes not long to decide. The soul acknowledges no difference, unless it be in favor of the latter. It was the first who led me on—oh, terrible consequences which have befallen me! It is so easy to blind those whom passion has already made dizzy! It is not wonderful that their converts are many. Why did not my dead mother come to me in her shroud, and warn me that not thus with miserable sophistries were the hearts of the happy and pure women of her day corrupted—that safety was only to be found in the straight and narrow path?

"Fondle your new mistress, Richard Wilde! make her ignobly happy for a week or month. The lips which only you ought to have pressed are dust; the voice of love unprofaned is forever silent. *I*, too, leave you, but not for the grave—would to God that it were! I leave you to your ambitious schemes; your mockery of religion; your unbridled desires. You will be a leading man among base men; you will fatten upon self-indulgence; your

conscience will grow easy and you will look upon
yourself with complacency. Even now you can
hide yourself from thoughts of your wife, buried
yesterday, in the arms of another woman; and I
have the consolation of knowing that I aided in
bringing you down to this.

"I have been selfish, sinful, infatuated; but if
suffering could expiate wrong-doing, I should come
out justified. I lay upon the bed of thorns which I
prepared for another. Did I not know, simpleton
that I was, that he would forsake me, as he had
done Margaret? Yes, I knew it, and yet I would
venture.

" What do you say to me, Margaret, out of your
lonely grave?" she asked, listening as if a spirit
spoke. " Always you came to me with gentle messages, full of truth and love. I must redeem the
past. If I have broken one heart, I must bind up
many that are bruised and bleeding. If I have led
one soul astray, I must win back many to the right.
I must give up seeking for happiness by living for
myself alone, and go forth and labor in the great
cause of humanity. Thus you whisper to me,
friend Margaret, and I will obey you. In life I

always gave you pain, but in death I will obey you. I will go back to the world, not proudly, but humbly, seeking only to do good. Always, always, my voice shall rise in defense of one love, constant through life, and faithful in death—one home—one father and mother for the children—one joy on earth —one hope in heaven. Always my spirit shall burn in defense of the purity of womanhood, against these specious pleaders, who would make it a thing of chance and change.

"I go; Margaret, farewell! I leave you to this solitude. And yet it is not you who are here; violets will grow out of your dust, but you are an angel, set in heaven like a star, to shine upon my future path."

She kissed the earth above Margaret, and hurried away. After a long walk she reached the city. Entering her house, she stole softly to her chamber. As she expected, there was no one there. She took from her bureau a small collection of valuables, and a purse full of gold which she fastened securely in her dress; returned down the stairs, went to the stable and saddled her pony, mounted him, and fled away through the midnight and the moonlight, leaving fortune and love behind.

At the close of the next day, the company with whom Harry and his wife were journeying, as they pitched their tents and cooked their suppers, were surprised by a woman riding into their midst. Sarah's tough little steed had done her good service in enabling her to overtake the travelers. Pale and weary, she dismounted, but before resting she went to Harry Fletcher.

"I wish to travel with this company until we reach the States," she said. "I have left Utah forever. A forlorn and unhappy woman, all I hope is to find some peace in works of good to others, and especially to my own sex. I have enough money to pay my way; and if you know how deeply humiliated I feel, you would not refuse to allow me to accompany you."

Harry looked upon the woman before him, her beauty all bowed down before her repentance, pale, sad-looking, making her request as meekly as a child. A vision of her past magnificent pride and loveliness swept before him—the contrast touched him deeply; but still it might have been impossible

20

for him to have emulated the forgiveness of his dead sister, had not Minnie, who stood regarding both, held out her hand to Sarah:

"Margaret loved and forgave you; can we do less?" she said. The tears which stood in her gentle eyes melted all the pride and anger which might have lingered in the hearts of the others.

So true it is that love which is like Christ's, unselfish, will soothe all the troubles, calm all the resentments, purify all the passions of humanity, and make brothers and sisters even of those who have avenged one another.

APPENDIX.

APPENDIX.

WHATEVER relates to the actual condition of Mormonism attracts attention, and deservedly; for now that Deseret has applied for admission to the Union it becomes us to learn all we can of the people and institutions with which we are to consort.

Of the population and the feeling of the people of Utah a late letter-writer from them says:

"The Indians in the Territory are said to be upward of twenty thousand, and the white population is usually estimated at some fifty to eighty thousand. But let me here say, in all candor, that this is believed by many to be a very low estimate. The fact is, emigration has come flowing in from all parts for several years, California, Australia, and the Pacific Isles contributing no small share. The country being healthy there are but few deaths; and there is one peculiarity which will soon have a great bearing on the population, viz., the utter annihilation of 'single blessedness' among this people. Every body is conscience-bound to marry as soon as they are old enough, and it is made a strict and conscientious duty, in the singular system which prevails here, for every family to raise all the children they can. If there was ever a country where an old bachelor would feel ashamed, it is here. I speak from experience; and as to old maids, they are out of the question; there is seldom, if ever, an unmarried female of twenty years old to be found in the Territory.

"There is no mistake but what the Mormons, at present rates, will ere long control several of the interior States and

21

Territories. There are three principal levers which constitute Mormon power as a body politic, viz.: First, an unanimity of action; Second, their peculiar institution of marriage and multiplication; Thirdly, the immense and well-concerted missionary system, which wields an influence over the whole globe. You Down Easters may laugh at them; theorists may speculate on Mormon dissoluteness, etc., but here they are a unit—and the spirit of union is increasing with them every year.

"For outward appearance' sake, and a decent respect for liberal institutions, they will go through all the forms, and apply in good earnest for an admission into the Union; but their real sentiments are that they do not care a fig whether they are admitted or not. They can not be but sensible that their path is onward to self-government and eventual independence, by whatever means this finale will be approached. And they are wise enough to 'bide their time.'"

Another writer says: "There is not a State in the world peopled by so heterogeneous a mass of human beings. There are many hundred Danes in Utah, Englishmen of all degrees of enlightenment and dialect, broad Yorkshire, Caernarvon Welsh, Dumfries Scotch, peasantry from the valleys of Switzerland, and deluded chamois hunters from her mountain peaks. There are Germans and Swedes, Sandwich Islanders, Hungarians and Poles; in fact all Europe, save the Russ and Moslem, are represented in this singularly peopled country."

A late English paper announcing the departure of emigrants for Utah, says: "On Wednesday last an extraordinary scene was witnessed at the New-street railway station. A fine ship, the *Enoch Train*, having been chartered to convey a cargo of Mormons to the United States, *en route* to their settlement in Utah Territory, three hundred men and women, boys and girls, formed the contingent supplied by the Birmingham district. They left by the half-past ten train. All seemed to belong to the working classes, and the proportion of the sexes was about equal. Many hundreds of their relatives and fellow-saints assembled at the station to bid them farewell; and, in spite of the efforts of an instrumental band to cheer the spirits of the females, some very affecting scenes were witnessed. There will be nine hundred on board."

The New York *Times*, of a late date, announcing the arrival of another ship load of emigrants, thus refers to them:

"The packet-ship *Caravan*, Captain Sands, arrived at this port on Thursday evening, from Liverpool, and landed her passengers at Castle Garden. They are four hundred and fifty-four in number, and are Mormons. They came from England, Wales, Scotland, Ireland, and Denmark. For the credit of Denmark there are only two Danish families among them. For the credit of Ireland there is only one Irishman.

"Our reporter saw these people, conversed with them, and estimated them, intellectually and otherwise. They all belong to the lower, almost to the lowest classes of society. The Welsh peasant is notably clean—these Welsh peasants were dirty. Very ruddy are the complexions of the Welsh girls, very wholesome their appearance, very staid and chaste their manners. The Welsh damsels our reporter saw yesterday, were neither ruddy, wholesome, nor staid. Further he will not testify. Some of them, a few months hence, will perhaps be added to Brigham Young's harem.

"Much has been said and written favorable to the European converts to Mormonism that was little deserved. The Mormon emigrants now at Castle Garden may be unfavorable specimens of their class. We were assured, however, by their leader, that they were considered not only respectable but wealthy. *They paid their own passage to America*, which Mormon converts seldom do wholly, even if they contribute in part to their expenses. They were regarded by their own people as rather aristocratic than otherwise. But what has been said of the Welsh is also true of the English and Scotch Mormons now at Castle Garden. Their countenances were imbruted with ignorance and dirt—not the material dirt of a sea voyage, but the moral dirt of a life of imbecility and indolence. The Apostles of Joe Smith and Brigham Young found them an easy prey, although, as our reporter was told, they were quite above the average of Mormon respectability.

"Among the whole four hundred and fifty, there was scarcely one face that showed that its possessor was greatly elevated above the animal. Dissipation had done its work with many. Most of the Englishmen had been evidently too familiar with the gin palaces and beer shops of London and the larger towns. The Scotchmen appeared to have drunk deep of whisky, and drunk themselves out of employment. If they paid their passages to this country, they must have had friends to send them out, as many fathers dispatch their prodigal sons to other lands, to get rid of them.

"We can not wonder how, with such intellects to work upon, Brigham Young's influence and power should extend. If Salt Lake City is wholly peopled by individuals of the average of intellect possessed by the newly-arrived emigrants, we should, following the law of depreciation, expect that in a century it would merely be a congregation of apes with tails."

From these items something may be gathered of the *character* of the population we are to deal with in Deseret. It is safe to say that the same kind of record as the above would answer for seven eighths of the people of that country, and, doubtless, will answer for the hordes now *en route* for this country, not only from Wales, and England and Scotland, but also from Scandinavia, where, by the following item it will be perceived they are strong both in effort and numbers:

"The Mormons have established a paper at Copenhagen, called the *Star of Scandinavia.* In this it is stated that the number of 'Latter Day Saints' in Denmark, Norway, and Sweden, amounts to 2,692 persons, among them are twenty-one elders, nineteen priests, fifteen teachers, and eleven deacons. In Sweden there are two hundred and forty Mormons. In Denmark 2,247, 1208 of whom are at Copenhagen."

If this is the character of the people, what can be the condition of morals at Salt Lake City. A few items clipped from late papers may serve to show. The following from the Salt Lake City *News* may be considered authentic:

"There is just complaint of the wickedness which is creeping into the brotherood of Saints. President Kimball, at the

Tabernacle, on the 24th of February, denounced it in the strongest style, saying that he would try and slay the man who would undertake to corrupt the people. He says; I am opposed to corruption; I wish every man to keep himself pure, whether he is Jew, or Gentile, or Latter-Day Saint; keep yourselves pure. I do not allow my women to fondle with other men, or to sit on their laps, and they must not suffer other men to hug and kiss them; if they do I will cast them off. Let my wives alone, and let my daughters alone, except you have my permission to pay them attention, and do as you wish to be done by. I am not afraid, for I am my heavenly Father's friend, and am a friend to all his sons and daughters, whether they make a profession of religion or not, but they must not undertake to pollute this people. I delight to have strangers come to my house, and they shall have the privilege of visiting and associating with me, and I associate with them on condition that they be like true gentlemen."

Another newspaper paragraph, from a late letter, reads: "Among the revolting features of Mormon institutions, that which permits marriage between blood relations, is the worst. He has met with numerous instances of men marrying both mother and daughter. A bishop of one of the wards married six wives, all sisters, and, moreover, his own nieces."

And to show still further the wretched and abject condition of women, let us quote from a late number of the Deseret *News*, the "Maxims for Mormon Wives:"

"1st. Occupy yourself only with household affairs; wait till your husband confides to you those of higher importance, and do not give your advice till he asks it.

"2d. Never take upon yourself to be a censor of your husband's morals, and do not read lectures to him. Let your preaching be a good example, and practice virtue yourself to make him in love with it.

"3d. Command his attention by being always attentive to him; never exact anything, and you will attain much; appear always flattered by the little he does for you, which will excite him to perform more.

"4th. All men are vain; never wound his vanity, not even in the most trifling instances. A wife may have more sense than her husband, but she should never seem to know it.

"5th. Seem always to obtain information from him, especially before company, though you may pass for a simpleton. Never forget that a wife owes all her importance to that of her husband."

Another exposition says: "Let our daughters also obey the ordinances of God, and receive and cultivate the gift of the Holy Ghost, in every good and pure affection. Let them early understand the true relationship they are destined to sustain to the other sex. Let them be taught to respect them as brothers, worthy of their confidence and affection—worthy to become their saviour and head, as Christ is the head of the church. Let them be taught to respect and revere themselves, as holy vessels destined to sustain and magnify the eternal and sacred relationship of wife and mother; to be the ornament and glory of man; and let them learn to respect themselves as sons of God; and the other sex as sisters—daughters of the Highest, holy vessels, eternal beings—destined as companions and co-workers in the great science of life. Let them be taught to aspire, by every principle of honor and integrity, to the patriarchal throne, as heads of families and saviours of men."

This is the people—these the institutions we are asked to admit to fellowship, and social and political equality: Are we prepared to accede to such a proposition?

BOOKS

PUBLISHED BY G. G. EVANS,

439 Chestnut St., Philadelphia.

T. S. ARTHUR'S WORKS.

The following Books are by T. S. ARTHUR, the well-known author, of whom it has been said, "that dying, he has not written a word he would wish to erase." They are worthy of a place in every household.

ARTHUR'S SKETCHES OF LIFE AND CHARACTER.

An octavo volume of over 400 pages, beautifully Illustrated, and bound in the best English muslin, gilt. Price $2.00.

LIGHTS AND SHADOWS OF REAL LIFE.

With an Autobiography and Portrait of the Author. Over 500 pages, octavo, with fine tinted Engravings. Price $2.00.

TEN NIGHTS IN A BAR-ROOM, AND WHAT I SAW THERE.

This powerfully-written work, one of the BEST by its POPULAR AUTHOR, has met with an immense sale. It is a large 12mo., illustrated with a beautiful Mezzotint Engraving, by Sartain; printed on fine white paper, and bound in the best English muslin, gilt back. Price, $1.00.

GOLDEN GRAINS FROM LIFE'S HARVEST-FIELD.

Bound in gilt back and sides, cloth, with a beautiful Mezzotint engraving. 12mo. Price $1.00.

WHAT CAN WOMAN DO.

12mo., with Mezzotint engraving. Price $1.00.

" Our purpose is to show, in a series of Life Pictures, what woman can do, as well for good as for evil."

ANGEL OF THE HOUSEHOLD, AND OTHER TALES.

Cloth, 12mo., with Mezzotint engraving. Price $1.00.

ARTHUR'S HOME LIBRARY.

[The following four volumes contain nearly 500 pages each, and are illustrated with fine Mezzotint engravings. Bound in the best manner, and sold separately or in sets. They have been introduced into the District, Sabbath School, and other Libraries, and are considered one of the best series of the Author.]

THREE ERAS IN WOMAN'S LIFE.

Containing Maiden, Wife and Mother. Cloth, 12mo., with Mezzotint engraving. Price, $1.00.

"This, by many, is considered Mr. Arthur's best work."

TALES OF MARRIED LIFE.

Containing Lovers and Husbands, Sweethearts and Wives, and Married and Single. Cloth, 12mo., with Mezzotint engraving. Price $1.00.

"In this volume may be found some valuable hints for wives and husbands, as well as for the young."

TALES OF REAL LIFE.

Containing Bell Martin, Pride and Principle, Mary Ellis, Family Pride and Alice Melville. Cloth, 12mo., with Mezzotint engraving. Price $1,00.

"This volume gives the experience of real life by many who found not their ideal."

THE MARTYR WIFE.

Containing Madeline, the Heiress, The Martyr Wife and Ruined Gamester. Cloth, 12mo., with Mezzotint engraving. $1.00.

"Contains several sketches of thrilling interest."

THE ANGEL AND THE DEMON.

A Book of Startling Interest. A handsome 12mo volume, $1.00.

"In this exciting story, Mr. Arthur has taken hold of the reader's attention with a more than usually vigorous grasp, and keeps him absorbed to the end of the volume."

THE WAY TO PROSPER,

AND OTHER TALES. Cloth, 12mo., with engraving. Price $1.00.

TRUE RICHES; OR WEALTH WITHOUT WINGS,

AND OTHER TALES. Cloth, 12mo., with Mezzotint engraving. Price, $1.00.

THE YOUNG LADY AT HOME.

A Series of Home Stories for American Women. 12mo. $1.00.

TRIALS AND CONFESSIONS OF A HOUSEKEEPER.

With 14 Spirited Illustrations. 12mo., cloth. Price $1.00.

The range of subjects in this book embrace the grave and instructive, as well as the agreeable and amusing. No Lady reader familiar with the trials and perplexities incident to Housekeeping, can fail to recognize many of her own experiences, for every picture here presented has been drawn from life.

THE WITHERED HEART.

With fine Mezzotint Frontispiece. 12mo., Cloth. Price $1.00.

This work has gone through several editions in England, although published but a short time, and has had the most flattering notices from the English Press.

STEPS TOWARD HEAVEN.

A Series of Lay Sermons for Converts in the Great Awakening. 12mo., cloth. Price $1.00.

THE HAND BUT NOT THE HEART;

Or, Life Trials of Jessie Loring. 12mo., cloth. Price, $1.00.

THE GOOD TIME COMING.

Large 12mo., with fine Mezzotint Frontispiece. Price, $1.00.

LEAVES FROM THE BOOK OF HUMAN LIFE.

Large 12mo. With 30 illustrations and steel plate. Price $1.00.

"It includes some of the best humorous sketches of the author."

HEART HISTORIES AND LIFE PICTURES.

12mo Cloth. Price $1.00.

"In the preparation of this volume, we have endeavored to show, that whatever tends to awaken our sympathies towards others, is an individual benefit as well as a common good."

SPARING TO SPEND; or, the Loftons and Pinkertons

12mo., cloth. Price $1.00.

The purpose of this volume is to exhibit the evils that flow from the too common lack of prudence.

HOME SCENES.

12mo. Cloth. Price $1.00.

This Book is designed to aid in the work of overcoming what is evil and selfish, that home lights may dispel home shadows.

THE OLD MAN'S BRIDE.

12mo. Cloth. Price $1.00.

This is a powerfully written Book, showing the folly of unequal marriages.

BIOGRAPHIES.

LIFE AND EXPLORATIONS OF DR. E. K. KANE,

And other Distinguished American Explorers. Including Ledyard, Wilkes, Perry, &c. Containing narratives of their researches and adventures in remote and interesting portions of the Globe. By Samuel M. Smucker, LL.D. With a fine Mezzotint Portrait of Dr. Kane, in his Arctic Costume. Price $1.00.

THE LIFE AND TIMES OF ALEXANDER HAMILTON.

By S. M. Smucker, LL.D. Large 12mo., with Portrait. Over 400 pages. Price $1.25.

THE LIFE AND TIMES OF THOMAS JEFFERSON.

By S. M. Smucker, LL.D., author of "Life and Reign of Nicholas I., Emperor of Russia," &c., &c. Large 12mo. of 400 pages. Cloth. With fine Steel Portrait. Price $1.25.

THE LIFE AND REIGN OF NICHOLAS I.,

Emperor of Russia. With descriptions of Russian Society and Government, and a full and complete History of the War in the East. Also, Sketches of Schamyl, the Circassian, and other Distinguished Characters. By S. M. Smucker, LL.D. Beautifully Illustrated. Over 400 pages, large 12mo. Price $1.25.

THE PUBLIC AND PRIVATE LIFE OF DANIEL WEBSTER.

By Gen. S. P. Lyman. 12mo., cloth. Price $1.00.

THE MASTER SPIRIT OF THE AGE.

THE PUBLIC AND PRIVATE HISTORY OF NAPOLEON THE THIRD.

With Biographical Notices of his most Distinguished Ministers, Generals and Favorites. By S. M. SMUCKER, LL.D. This interesting and valuable work is embellished with splendid steel plates, done by Sartain in his best style, including the Emperor, the Empress, Queen Hortense, and the Countess Castiglione. 400 pages, 12mo. Price $1.25.

MEMOIRS OF ROBERT HOUDIN,

The celebrated French Conjuror. Translated from the French. With a copious Index. By DR. R. SHELTON MACKENZIE. This book is full of interesting and entertaining anecdotes of the great Wizard, and gives descriptions of the manner of performing many of his most curious tricks and transformations. 12mo., cloth. Price $1.00.

LIFE AND ADVENTURES OF DAVID CROCKETT.

Written by himself, with Notes and Additions. Splendidly illustrated with engravings, from original designs. By GEORGE G. WHITE. 12mo., cloth. Price $1.00.

LIFE AND TIMES OF DANIEL BOONE.

Including an account of the Early Settlements of Kentucky. By CECIL B. HARTLEY. With splendid illustrations, from original drawings by George G. White. 12mo., cloth. Price $1.00.

LIFE AND ADVENTURES OF LEWIS WETZEL.

Together with Biographical Sketches of Simon Kenton, Benjamin Logan, Samuel Brady, Isaac Shelby, and other distinguished Warriors and Hunters of the West. By CECIL B. HARTLEY. With splendid illustrations, from original drawings by George G. White. 12mo., cloth. Price $1.00.

LIFE AND TIMES OF GENERAL FRANCIS MARION,

The Hero of the American Revolution; giving full accounts of his many perilous adventures and hair-breadth escapes amongst the British and Tories in the Southern States, during the struggle for liberty. By W. GILMORE SIMMS. 12mo., cloth. $1.00.

LIFE OF GENERAL SAMUEL HOUSTON,

The Hunter, Patriot, and Statesman of Texas. With nine ill
trations. 12mo., cloth. Price $1.00.

LIVES OF GENERAL HENRY LEE AND GENER/ THOMAS SUMPTER.

Comprising a History of the War in the Southern Department
the United States. Illustrated, 12mo, cloth. $1.00.

DARING & HEROIC DEEDS OF AMERICAN WOME

Comprising Thrilling Examples of Courage, Fortitude, Devot
ness, and Self-Sacrifice, among the Pioneer Mothers of
Western Country. By JOHN FROST, LL.D. Price $1.00.

LIVES OF FEMALE MORMONS.

A Narrative of facts Stranger than Fiction. By METTA VICTO
FULLER. 12mo., cloth. Price $1.00.

LIVES OF ILLUSTRIOUS WOMEN OF ALL AGES.

Containing the Empress Josephine, Lady Jane Gray, Beat
Cenci, Joan of Arc, Anne Boleyn, Charlotte Corday, Zenob
&c., &c. Embellished with Fine Steel Portraits. 12mo., clo
Price $1.00.

THE LIVES AND EXPLOITS OF THE MOST NOTI BUCCANEERS & PIRATES OF ALL COUNTRIES.

Handsomely illustrated. 1 vol. Cloth. Price $1.00.

HIGHWAYMEN, ROBBERS AND BANDITTI OF A COUNTRIES.

With Colored and other Engravings. Handsomely bound in
volume. 12mo., cloth. Price $1.00.

HEROES AND PATRIOTS OF THE SOUTH;

Comprising Lives of General Francis Marion, General Willi
Moultrie, General Andrew Pickens, and Governor J
Rutledge. By CECIL B. HARTLEY. Illustrated, 12mo., clo
Price $1.00.

THE PRINCE

OF THE

HOUSE OF DAVID;

OR,

THREE YEARS IN THE HOLY CITY.

BEING

A SERIES OF THE LETTERS OF ADINA, A JEWESS OF ALEXANDRIA, SUPPOSED
TO BE SOJOURNING IN JERUSALEM IN THE DAYS OF HEROD,
ADDRESSED TO HER FATHER, A WEALTHY JEW IN EGYPT,

AND RELATING, AS IF BY AN EYE-WITNESS,

ALL THE SCENES AND WONDERFUL INCIDENTS

IN THE

LIFE OF JESUS OF NAZARETH,

FROM HIS

Baptism in Jordan to his Crucifixion on Calvary.

NEW EDITION, CAREFULLY REVISED AND CORRECTED BY THE AUTHOR,

REV. J. H. INGRAHAM, LL. D.

Rector of Christ Church, and of St. Thomas' Hall, Holly Springs, Miss.

WITH FIVE SPLENDID ILLUSTRATIONS.

ONE LARGE 12mo. VOLUME, CLOTH, $1.25.

THE SAME WORK IN GERMAN. One volume 12mo.,
cloth.   PRICE $1.00

THE PILLAR OF FIRE;

OR,

ISRAEL IN BONDAGE.

BEING AN ACCOUNT OF THE

WONDERFUL SCENES IN THE LIFE OF THE SON OF PHARAOH'S DAUGHTER, (MOSES.)

TOGETHER WITH

PICTURESQUE SKETCHES OF THE HEBREWS UNDER THEIR TASK-MASTERS.

BY REV. J. H. INGRAHAM, LL.D.,

Author of the "Prince of the House of David."

PRICE, $1.25.

"THE PILLAR OF FIRE," is a large 12mo. volume of 600 pages, Illustrated, and contains an account of the wonderful scenes in the life of the Son of Pharaoh's Daughter, (Moses,) from his youth to the ascent of Sinai: comprising as by an eye-witness, his Miracles before Pharaoh, Passage of the Red Sea, and the reception of the Law on Mount Sinai, &c., &c.

RECORDS OF THE REVOLUTIONARY WAR.

Containing the Military and Financial Correspondence of distinguished officers; names of the officers and privates of regiments, companies and corps, with the dates of their commissions and enlistments. General orders of Washington, Lee, and Green; with a list of distinguished prisoners of war; the time of their capture, exchange, etc.; to which is added the half-pay acts of the Continental Congress; the Revolutionary pension laws; and a list of the officers of the Continental army who acquired the right to half-pay, commutation, and lands, &c. By T. W. SAFFELL. Large 12mo., $1.25.

THE ROMANCE OF THE REVOLUTION.

Being a history of the personal adventures, romantic incidents and exploits incidental to the War of Independence—with tinted illustrations. Large 12mo., $1.25.

THE QUEEN'S FATE.

A tale of the days of Herod. 12mo., cloth, with Steel Illustrations. $1.00.

"A recital of events, of an awe-arousing period, in a familiar and interesting manner."

"LIVING AND LOVING."

A collection of Sketches. By MISS VIRGINIA F. TOWNSEND.— Large 12mo., with fine steel portrait of the author. Bound in cloth. Price $1.00.

We might say many things in favor of this delightful publication, but we deem it unnecessary. Husbands should buy it for their wives: lovers should buy it for their sweet-hearts: friends should buy it for their friends.—*Godey's Lady's Book.*

WHILE IT WAS MORNING.

By VIRGINIA F. TOWNSEND, author of "Living and Loving." 12mo., cloth. Price $1.00.

THE ANGEL VISITOR ; OR, VOICES OF THE HEART.

12mo., cloth, with Mezzotint Engraving. Price $1.00.

"The mission of this volume is to aid in doing good to those in affliction."

THE SPIRIT LAND.

12mo., cloth, with Mezzotint Engraving.   Price $1.00.

"These pages are submitted to the public with the counsel of the wisest and best of all ages, that amid the wiley arts of the Adversary, we should cling to the word of GOD, the Bible, as the only safe and infallible guide of Faith and Practice."

THE MORNING STAR; OR, SYMBOLS OF CHRIST.

By REV WM. M. THAYER, author of "Hints for the Household," "Pastor's Holiday Gift," &c., &c.   12mo., cloth.   Price $1.00.

"The symbolical parts of Scriptures are invested with peculiar attractions. A familiar acquaintance with them can scarcely fail to increase respect and love for the Bible."

SWEET HOME; OR, FRIENDSHIP'S GOLDEN ALTAR.

By FRANCES C. PERCIVAL.   Mezzotint Frontispiece, 12mo., cloth, gilt back and centre.   Price $1.00.

"The object of this book is to awaken the Memories of Home—to remind us of the old Scenes and old Times."

THE DESERTED FAMILY;

OR, THE WANDERINGS OF AN OUTCAST.   By PAUL CREYTON.   12mo., cloth.   Price $1.00.

"An interesting story, which might exert a good influence in softening the heart, warming the affections, and elevating the soul."

ANNA CLAYTON; OR, THE MOTHER'S TRIAL.

A Tale of Real Life.   12mo., cloth.   Price $1.00.

"The principal characters in this tale are drawn from real life—imagination cannot picture deeper shades of sadness, higher or more exquisite joys, than *Truth* has woven for us, in the Mother's Trial."

"FASHIONABLE DISSIPATION."

By METTA V. FULLER.   Mezzotint Frontispiece, 12mo., bound in cloth,   Price $1.00.

"TO THE PURE ALL THINGS ARE PURE."

WOMAN AND HER DISEASES.

From the Cradle to the Grave ; adapted exclusively to her instruction in the Physiology of her system, and all the Diseases of her Critical Periods. By EDWARD H. DIXON, M.D. 12mo. Price $1.00.

DR. LIVINGSTONE'S TRAVELS AND RESEARCHES OF SIXTEEN YEARS IN THE WILDS OF SOUTH AFRICA.

One volume, 12mo., cloth, fine edition, printed upon superior paper, with numerous illustrations. Price $1.25. Cheap edition, price $1.00.

This is a work of thrilling adventures and hair-breadth escapes among savage beasts, and more savage men. Dr. Livingstone was alone, and unaided by any white man, traveling only with African attendants, among different tribes and nations, all strange to him, and many of them hostile, and altogether forming the most astonishing book of travels the world has ever seen. All acknowledge it is the most readable book published.

ANDERSSON'S EXPLORATIONS AND DISCOVERIES.

Giving accounts of many Perilous Adventures, and Thrilling Incidents, during Four Years' Wanderings in the Wilds of South Western Africa. By C. J. ANDERSSON, LL.D., F.R.S. With an Introductory Letter, by J. C. FREMONT. One volume, 12mo., cloth. With Numerous Illustrations, representing Sporting Adventures, Subjects of Natural History, Devices for Destroying Wild Animals, etc. Price $1.25.

INDIA AND THE INDIAN MUTINY.

Comprising a Complete History of Hindoostan, from the earliest times to the present day, with full particulars of the Recent Mutiny in India. Illustrated with numerous engravings. By HENRY FREDERICK MALCOM. This work has been gotten up with great care, and may be relied on as Complete and Accurate ; making one of the most Thrillingly Interesting books published. It contains illustrations of all the great Battles and Sieges, making a large 12mo., volume of about 450 pages. Price $1.25.

SEVEN YEARS IN THE WILDS OF SIBERIA,

A Narrative of Seven Years' Explorations and Adventures in Oriental and Western Siberia, Mongolia, the Kir his Steppes, Chinese Tartary, and Part of Central Asia. By THOMAS WILLIAM ATKINSON. With numerous Illustrations. 12mo., cloth, price $1.25.

SIX YEARS IN NORTHERN AND CENTRAL AFRICA.

Travels and Discoveries in North and Central Africa, being a Journal of an Expedition undertaken under the auspices of H. B. M.'s Government, in the years 1849-1855. By HENRY BARTH, Ph. D., D.C.L., Fellow of the Royal Geographical and Asiatic Societies, &c., &c. 12mo., cloth, price $1.25.

THREE VISITS TO MADAGASCAR

During the years 1853, 1854, 1856, including a journey to the Capital; with notices of the Natural History of the Country and of the present Civilization of the People, by the Rev. WM. ELLIS, F.H.S., author of "Polynesian Researches." Illustrated by engravings from photographs, &c. 12mo., cloth. $1.25.

CAPT. COOK'S VOYAGES ROUND THE WORLD.

One volume, 12mo., cloth.   Price $1.00.

BOOK OF ANECDOTES AND BUDGET OF FUN.

Containing a collection of over One Thousand Laughable Sayings, Rich Jokes, etc. 12mo., cloth, extra gilt back, $1.00.

"Nothing is so well calculated to preserve the healthful action of the human system as a good hearty laugh."

BOOK OF PLAYS FOR HOME AMUSEMENT.

Being a collection of Original, Altered and well-selected Tragedies, Comedies, Dramas, Farces, Burlesques, Charades, Comic Lectures, etc. Carefully arranged and specially adapted for PRIVATE REPRESENTATION, with full directions for Performance. By SILAS S. STEELE, Dramatist. One volume, 12mo., cloth. Price $1.00.

A HISTORY OF ITALY,

AND THE WAR OF 1859.

Giving the causes of the War, with Biographical Sketches of Sovereigns, Statesmen and Military Commanders; Descriptions and Statistics of the Country; with finely engraved Portraits of Louis Napoleon, Emperor of France Frances Joseph, Emperor of Austria; Victor Emanuel, King of Sardinia, and Garribaldi, the Champion of Italian Freedom. Together with the official accounts of the Battles of Montebello, Palestro, Magenta, Malegnano, Solferino, etc., etc., and Maps of Italy, Austria, and all the adjacent Countries, by

MADAME JULIE DE MARGUERITTES.

With an introduction by Dr. R. Shelton Mackenzie, one volume, 12mo., cloth, price $1.25.

From the New York Courier and Enquirer.

" This is an able, interesting and lively account of the War and the circumstances connected with it. The author's residence in Europe has given her facilities for preparing the volume which add much to its value.

"Not only does she give a description of Italy in general, but of each Sovereignty, and State, showing the Extent, Resources, Power and Political situation of each. Throughout the volume are found Anecdotes, Recollections, and even *Ondits*, which contribute to its interest."

THE BOOK OF POPULAR SONGS.

Being a compendium of the best Sentimental, Comic, Negro, National, Patriotic, Military, Naval, Social, Convivial, and Pathetic Ballads and Melodies, as sung by the most celebrated Opera Singers, Negro Minstrels, and Comic Vocalists of the day. One volume, 12mo., cloth.   Price $1.00.

THE AMERICAN PRACTICAL COOKERY BOOK;

Or, Housekeeping made easy, pleasant, and econmical in all its departments. To which are added directions for setting out Tables, and giving Entertainments. Directions for Jointing, Trussing, and Carving, and many hundred new Receipts in Cookery and Housekeeping. With 50 engravings. 12mo., cloth.   Price $1.00.

A BUDGET OF

HUMOROUS POETRY,

COMPRISING

Specimens of the best and most Humorous Productions of the
popular American and Foreign Poetical Writers of the day.
By the author of the "BOOK OF ANECDOTES AND BUDGET OF
FUN." One volume, 12mo., cloth.   Price $1.00.

From the Philadelphia North American.

"This collection includes specimens of the Humorous Writings of English
and American authors, and the preference is given to contemporaries. The
compiler has aimed to produce a volume in which every piece should provoke
'a good hearty laugh.' In one thing he has certainly shown a wisdom which
might be imitated by compilers of more pretension. He does not claim that his
work represents the 'entire humorous literature of the language,' but a collection of poetical effusions, replete with wit and humor."

THE

The World in a Pocket Book.

BY

WILLIAM H. CRUMP.

NEW AND REVISED EDITION, BROUGHT DOWN TO

1860.

This work is a Compendium of Useful Knowledge and General
Reference, dedicated to the Manufacturers, Farmers, Merchants,
and Mechanics of the United States—to all, in short, with whom
time is money—and whose business avocations render the acqui-
sition of extensive and diversified information desirable, by the
shortest possible road.   This volume, it is hoped, will be found
worthy of a place in every household—in every family.   It
may indeed be termed a library in itself.   Large 12mo., $1.25.

THE

LADIES' HAND BOOK

OF

FANCY AND ORNAMENTAL

NEEDLE-WORK,

COMPRISING

FULL DIRECTIONS WITH PATTERNS

FOR WORKING IN

Embroidery, Applique, Braiding, Crochet, Knitting, Netting,
Tatting, Quilting, Tambour and Gobelin Tapestry,
Broderie Anglaise, Guipure Work, Canvass Work,
Worsted Work, Lace Work, Bead Work,
Stitching, Patch Work, Frivolite,
etc., etc., etc.

ILLUSTRATED WITH 262 ENGRAVED PATTERNS,

TAKEN FROM ORIGINAL DESIGNS.

BY MISS FLORENCE HARTLEY.

ONE VOLUME, QUARTO CLOTH, Price $1.25.

LECTURES for the PEOPLE:

BY THE

REV. H. STOWELL BROWN,

Of the Myrtle Street Baptist Chapel, Liverpool, England.

FIRST SERIES,

PUBLISHED UNDER A SPECIAL ARRANGEMENT WITH THE AUTHOR.

WITH A BIOGRAPHICAL INTRODUCTION BY

DR. R. SHELTON MACKENZIE.

WITH A SPLENDIDLY ENGRAVED STEEL PORTRAIT.

One Volume, 414 pages, 12mo. Cloth.   Price $1.00.

CONTENTS OF "LECTURES FOR THE PEOPLE."

1	The Lord's Prayer.	11	Saturday Night.
2	The Golden Rule.	12	There's nae Luck about the House.
3	The Prodigal Son.		
4	There's a good time coming.	13	The road to Hell is paved with good Intentions.
5	Turning over a new leaf.		
6	Taking care of Number One.	14	Poor Richard's Almanac.
7	Penny Wise and Pound Foolish.	15	Waste not, Want not.
8	Cleanliness is next to Godliness.	16	Tell the Truth and Shame the Devil.
9	A Friend in need is a Friend Indeed.	17	The Seventh Commandment.
		18--19	The Street.
		20	Stop Thief.
10	Five Shillings and Costs.	21	The Devil's Meal is all Bran.

Mr. Brown's lectures fill an important place, for which we have no other book. The style is clear, the spirit is kind, the reasoning careful, and the argument conclusive. We are persuaded that this book will render more good than any book of sermons or lectures that have been published in this 19th century.—*Liverpool Mercury.*

LIGHTS AND SHADOWS OF A PASTOR'S LIFE.

By S. H. Elliott. One volume, 12mo., cloth. Price $1.00.

" This is a well-written, highly instructive book. It is a story of the life-teachings, and life-trials of a good man, whose great aim was to elevate, morally and intellectually, his fellow-men. Like many of his nature and temperament, some of his views were Utopian. But his successes and failures, with the causes of these, are painted with a masterly hand. There is unusual strength and vitality in this volume."

THREE PER CENT. A MONTH;

Or, the Perils of Fast Living. A Warning to Young Men. By Chas. Burdett. One volume, 12mo., cloth. Price $1.00.

"The style of this book is direct and effective, particularly fitting the impression which such a story should make. It is a very spirited and instructive tale, leaving a good impression both upon the reader's sensibilities and morals."

EVENINGS AT HOME;

Or, Tales for the Fireside. By Jane C. Campbell. One volume, 12mo., cloth. Price $1.00.

" We know of no book in the whole range of modern fictitious literature we would sooner select for a delightful and instructive companion."

RURAL LIFE;

Or, Prose and Poetry of the Woods and Fields. By Harry Penciller. One volume, cloth, 12mo. Price $1.00.

" Beautiful landscapes, family scenes and conversations, rural sketches of woods and vales, of the beauties of verdant fields and fragrant flowers, of the music of birds and running brooks, all described in an original and un-studied manner, which cannot fail to delight every one whose character is imbued with a love of nature."

JOYS AND SORROWS OF HOME;

An Autobiography. By Anna Leland. One volume, 12mo., cloth. Price $1.00

" This is one of the most beautiful domestic stories we have ever read, intensely interesting, with a natural flow and easiness which leads the reader imperceptibly on to the close, and then leaves a regret that the tale is done."

2*

BEAUTY OF WOMAN'S FAITH;

A Tale of Southern Life. One volume, 12mo., cloth. Price $1 00.

" This volume contains the story of a French Emigrant, who first escaped to England, and afterward settled on a plantation in Louisiana. It is charmingly told, and the strength and endurance of woman's faith well illustrated."

THE ORPHAN BOY;

Or, Lights and Shadows of Northern Life. By Jeremy Loud. One volume, 12mo., cloth. Price $1.00.

"This is a work illustrating the passions and pleasures, the trials and triumphs of common life; it is well written and the interest is admirably sustained."

THE ORPHAN GIRLS;

A Tale of Life in the South. By James S. Peacock, M.D., of Mississippi. One volume, 12mo., cloth. Price $1.00.

"The style is fluent and unforced, the description of character well limned, and the pictures of scenery forcible and felicitous. There is a natural conveyance of incidents to the *dénouement*, and the reader closes the volume with an increased regard for the talent and spirit of the author."

NEW ENGLAND BOYS;

Or, the Three Apprentices. By A. L. Stimson. One volume, 12mo., Cloth. Price $1 00.

" This is a very agreeable book, written in a dashing independent style. The incidents are numerous and striking, the characters life-like, and the plot sufficiently captivating to enchain the reader's attention to the end of the volume."

THE KING'S ADVOCATE;

Or, the Adventures of a Witch Finder. One volume, 12mo., cloth. Price $1.00.

"This is a book so thoroughly excellent, so exalted in its character, so full of exquisite pictures of society, and manifesting so much genius, skill. and knowledge of human nature, that no one can possibly read it without admitting it to be, in every way, a noble book. The story, too, is one of stirring interest; and it either sweeps you along with its powerful spell, or beguiles you with its tenderness, pathos and geniality."

SIBYL MONROE; OR, THE FORGER'S DAUGHTER.

By MARTHA RUSSELL. One volume, 12mo., cloth. Price $1.00.

" It is a spirited, charming story, full of adventure, friendship and love, with characters nicely drawn and carefully discriminated. The clear style and spirit with which the story is presented and the characters developed, will attract a large constituency to the perusal."

THE OPEN BIBLE;

As shown in the History of Christianity, from the time of our Saviour to the Present Day. By VINCENT W. MILLNER. With a view of the latest developments of Rome's hostility to the Bible, as exhibited in the Sandwich Islands, in Tuscany, in Ireland, France, &c., and an expose of the absurdities of the Immaculate Conception, and the Idolatrous Veneration of the Virgin Mary. By REV. JOSEPH F. BERG, D. D., author of "The Jesuits," "Church and State," &c., &c. Illustrated with numerous Engravings. 12mo., cloth, gilt back. Price $1.00.

LIFE OF CHRIST AND HIS APOSTLES.

By the REV. JOHN FLEETWOOD. With a History of the Jews, from the Earliest Period to the Present Time. Large 12mo., bound in Cloth. Illustrated. Price $1.00.
Octavo edition, with steel engravings. Turkey Antique, $3.50.

BUNYAN'S PILGRIM'S PROGRESS.

Including, "Grace abounding to the Chief of Sinners." Large 12mo., 500 pages. Cloth. Beautifully Illustrated. Price $1.00.
Octavo edition, with steel engravings. Turkey Antique, $3.50.

SCRIPTURE EMBLEMS AND ALLEGORIES.

Being a series of Emblematic Engravings, with explanations and religious reflections, designed to illustrate Divine Truth. By REV. W. HOLMES. 12mo., cloth. Price $1.25.

HOME MEMORIES;

OR, SOCIAL HALF HOURS WITH THE HOUSEHOLD.
Octavo, 400 pages. Illustrated with fine steel plates. Cloth, Price $2.00. Turkey Antique, $3.50.

EVANS' POPULAR SPEAKER,

LYCEUM AND SCHOOL EXHIBITION DECLAIMER.

Comprising a Treatise on Elocution and Gesture, with Illustrations, and a choice collection of pieces in Prose and Verse, and selec. Dialogues, specially adapted for School and Lyceum Exhibitions, and Private Representations. 12mo., cloth.   Price $1.00.

PANORAMA OF THE OLD WORLD AND THE NEW;

Comprising a view of the present state of the Nations of the World, their Names, Customs and Peculiarities, and their Political, Moral, Social and Industrial Condition. Interspersed with Historical Sketches and Anecdotes.   By WILLIAM PINNOCK, author of the Histories of England, Greece and Rome. Enlarged, revised and embellished with several hundred Engravings, including twenty-four finely colored Plates, from designs by Croome, Devereux, and other distinguished artists.   In one vol. Octavo, over 600 pages, bound in embossed morocco, gilt back. Price $2.75.

GREAT EVENTS IN MODERN HISTORY.

Comprising the most remarkable Discoveries, Conquests, Revolutions, Great Battles and other Thrilling Incidents, chiefly in Europe and America, from the commencement of the Sixteenth Century to the Present Time.   By JOHN FROST, LL.D.   Embellished with over 500 engravings, by Croome and other eminent artists.   With a Map of the World, 20 by 25 inches, with side Maps of California, Oregon, Hungary, Austrian Dominions, &c. Royal Octavo over 800 pages, bound in embossed morocco, gilt back.   Price $3.00.

HUNTING SCENES IN THE WILDS OF AFRICA.

Comprising the Thrilling Adventures of Cumming, Harris, and other daring Hunters of Lions, Elephants, Giraffes, Buffaloes, and other Animals.   With Illustrations. 12mo., cloth.   Gilt back.   Price $1.00.

THE BATTLE FIELDS OF THE REVOLUTION.

Comprising descriptions of the Different Battles, Sieges, and other Events of the War of Independence. Interspersed with Characteristic Anecdotes. Illustrated with numerous Engravings, and a fine Mezzotint Frontispiece. By THOMAS Y. RHOADS. Large 12mo., cloth. Price $1.25.

PERILS AND PLEASURES OF A HUNTER'S LIFE.

With fine colored plates. Large 12mo., cloth. Price $1.25.
From the table of contents we take the following as samples of the style and interest of the work :
Baiting for an Alligator—Morning among the Rocky Mountains—Encounter with Shoshonees—A Grizzly Bear—Fight and terrible result—Fire on the Mountains—Narrow Escape —The Beaver Region—Trapping Beaver—A Journey and Hunt through New Mexico—Start for South America—Hunting in the Forests of Brazil—Hunting on the Pampas—A Hunting Expedition into the interior of Africa—Chase of the Rhinoceros—Chase of an Elephant—The Roar of the Lion—Herds of Wild Elephants—Lions attacked by Bechuanas—Arrival in the Region of the Tiger and the Elephant—Our first Elephant Hunt in India—A Boa Constrictor—A Tiger—A Lion—Terrible Conflict—Elephant Catching—Hunting the Tiger with Elephants—Crossing the Pyrenees—Encounter with a Bear—A Pigeon Hunt on the Ohio—A Wild Hog Hunt in Texas— Hunting the Black-tailed Deer.

THRILLING ADVENTURES AMONG THE INDIANS.

By JOHN FROST, LL.D. Comprising the most remarkable Personal Narratives of Events in the Early Indian Wars, as well as of Incidents in the recent Indian Hostilities in Mexico and Texas. Illustrated with over 300 engravings, from designs by W. Croome, and other distinguished artists. It contains over 500 pages. 12mo., cloth. Gilt back, $1.25.

PIONEER LIFE IN THE WEST.

Comprising the Adventures of Boone, Kenton, Brady, Clarke, the Whetzels, and others, in their Fierce Encounters with the Indians. With Illustrations, 12mo., cloth. Gilt back. Price $1.00.

McCULLOUGH'S TEXAN RANGERS.

The Scouting Expedition of McCullough's Texan Rangers, including Skirmishes with the Mexicans, and an accurate detail of the Storming of Monterey, &c., with Anecdotes, Incidents and Description of the Country, and Sketches of the lives of Hays, McCullough and Walker. By S. C. Reid, Jr., of Louisiana, late of the Texan Rangers. 12mo., cloth. Price $1.00.

THE DOOMED CHIEF.

Or, Two Hundred Years Ago. A Narrative of the Earliest Border Warfare. By D. B. Thompson, author of " Gaut Gurley," &c. 12mo., cloth. $1.00.

HUNTING SPORTS IN THE WEST.

Containing Adventures of the most celebrated Hunters and Trappers of the West. Illustrated with new designs. 12mo., cloth. $1.00.

GAUT GURLEY;

Or, the Trappers of Umbagog. A Tale of Border Life. By D. B. Thompson, author of " The Rangers ; or, the Tory's Daughter," " Green Mountain Boys," &c. 12mo., cloth. Price $1 00.

THE RECOLLECTIONS OF A SOUTHERN MATRON.

By Mrs. Caroline Gilman, of South Carolina. 12mo., cloth. Price $1.00.

"This volume is one of those books which are read by all classes at all stages of life, with an interest which looses nothing by change or circumstances."

THE ENCHANTED BEAUTY.

And other Tales and Essays. By Dr. Wm. Elder. 12mo., cloth. Price $1.00.

" This is a volume of beautiful and cogent essays, virtuous in motive, simple in expression, pertinent and admirable in logic, and glorious in conclusion and climax."

THE CHILD'S FAIRY BOOK.

By Spencer W. Cone. Containing a choice collection of beautiful Fairy Tales. Illustrated with Ten Beautiful Engravings, Splendidly Colored. 12mo., cloth. Price $1.00.